GROW A PAIR OF ANTLERS

COURAGEOUS · INFLUENTIAL · INTENTIONAL ·

THE FEARLESS DOE EDITION

THE FEARLESS CLIMB TO LEAD YOUR HERD

KATHLEEN RIES-JUBENVILLE

Grow a Pair of Antlers: The Fearless Climb to Lead Your Herd
The Fearless Doe Edition

Dedicated to my amazing children, Kaitlyn and John, and wonderful niece and nephew, Eliese and Alec.

May your lives be filled with love and inspired by hope, curiosity, and courage.

Thank you to my loving parents, Don and Diane, and my devoted husband, Ed, who have always encouraged and supported my dreams.

In loving memory of my brother, Dan, and with great respect and appreciation for the men and women who serve our country and defend our freedom.

Foreword

As a coach, I am honored to work with dozens of individuals, each unique in their gifts and contribution to the world in which they live. I am blessed to be able to help people figure out their passions in life, and organize an approach to achieving their goals and dreams without sacrificing the other priorities in their life. If fact, I have found that people who focus, holistically and sustainably, on their unique priorities, while also dreaming BIG dreams and methodically pursuing their ambitious goals – these are the people who can indeed "have it all." It is not necessary to sacrifice one side of your life (family, health, faith, emotions, meaning) in order to achieve massive success in business, finances, or other areas. People who figure this out are not only living better lives, but they also tend to be the ones who help other people live their best lives. They are eager to share their secrets, and are believers in abundance and the blessings that come from genuinely helping other people. They become our mentors, teachers, coaches and guides.

While I have been "coaching" Kathleen Ries-Jubenville for many months, I am also the one who is being coached through her unique strengths and zest for life. Having overcome an incredible set of personal challenges, and through faith, persistence, courage and grit, Kathleen has shown that it is possible to achieve tremendous success while staying true to a core set of timeless principles. In this book, "Grow a Pair of Antlers," Kathleen shares her unique perspective, aimed primarily at women (but equally applicable to men) on how to orient oneself and then grow in personal capability and also as a leader.

The world is in great need of more exceptional leaders, both women and men, and this book is a "must-read" resource for all who have the ambition to lead well while living their best lives.

Brett A. Blair
Author of "From Autopilot to Authentic"

Table of Contents

"The High Places," answered the Shepherd, "are the starting places for the journey down to the lowest place in the world. When you have hinds' feet and can go 'leaping on the mountains and skipping on the hills,' you will be able, as I am, to run down from the heights in the gladdest self-giving and then go up to the mountains again. You will be able to mount to the High Places swifter than eagles, for it is only up on the High Places of Love that anyone can receive the power to pour themselves down in utter abandonment of self-giving."

— *Hinds' Feet on High Places*, Hannah Hurnard

"The Lord God is my strength, and he will make my feet like hinds' feet, and he will make me to walk upon mine high places."

— *Habakkuk 3:19, The Holy Bible, KJV*

Who is a Fearless Doe?

A FEARLESS DOE is a passionate visionary whose intentional purpose is to enhance other people's lives. She takes courageous actions to foster dignity for others through inspiration and opportunity. She is an influential leader who promotes love, respect, grace, and hope.

A Fearless Doe understands that personal wealth is a wonderful goal, but it is not a fulfilling mission for her life. Making money is important to a Fearless Doe, but providing opportunity for others is her focus and her passion. That is why you will recognize a Fearless Doe by the success of the people who are influenced by her, not by the color of her nails or height of her heels.

A Fearless Doe builds companies, produces art or creative ideas, and leads people. She always pursues personal growth and innovation. She draws upon faith and fellowship to courageously face risks and engender change.

A Fearless Doe can be any shape, color, or age because she uses her gifts and talents to impact the world through the passion of her vision and confidence in her life experience and wisdom.

A Fearless Doe doesn't accept the negative thoughts that

attempt to flood her mind. She fights them off and focuses on gratitude and hard work. She looks for and appreciates the beauty and joy all around her in the world.

A Fearless Doe is an optimist. She may have survived tremendous challenges in her past, but she is resilient. She is a bold survivor who believes in a greater purpose. She understands life has ups and downs and faces it bravely with her head held high. She allows herself to feel hopeful and loved.

A Fearless Doe respects all people's freedom of choice and expression, but sets high standards for performance. She clearly communicates her expectations and helps her family or team succeed in achieving them.

A Fearless Doe understands everyone has a story, a personal struggle, so she does not easily take offense. She has compassion for those who feel the need to lash out or defend themselves. But she sets relationship limits to protect her positive energy.

A Fearless Doe does the best she can with what she knows and what she has right now. She believes in responsibility and opportunity. She hasn't given up yet and doesn't intend to. She proactively sets challenging goals and pursues her dreams.

A Fearless Doe exemplifies good moral character, demonstrates a positive attitude, and pursues mastery of the skills of Intentional Purpose, Courageous Actions, and Influential Leadership.

Preface

Hi, I'm Kathleen Ries-Jubenville, author of this book, "Grow a Pair of Antlers: The Fearless Climb to Lead Your Herd." I have been a student of personal growth since my early twenties. My journey began when I first listened to the audiobook "Awaken the Giant Within" by performance expert Tony Robbins. His powerful message instilled in me the belief that I can exert significant control over my emotions and my destiny. As a result, I have actively and strategically pursued challenging opportunities in my career to develop expertise in business finance, management and leadership. For twelve years, I worked for an international corporation to learn how the "big guys" achieve financial success. During this time, I attended college classes in the evenings and on the weekends to earn my bachelor's degree in business finance. I then started my own accounting consulting firm to teach small business owners professional standards of excellence and assist them in implementing streamlined operational systems. I have helped hundreds of entrepreneurs establish and expand their business ventures and increase their profitability. I enjoy the work of helping people achieve their dreams so much, I decided to write this book to serve people exponentially. I poured my life's passions, values and experiences into this book. As you will discover, I include many of my beliefs in these pages. I am Christian and share wisdom from and thoughts about my faith. However, this is not intended to be a book only for Christians. It is for every woman on her journey of personal growth and, ultimately, leadership and service to others. My goal is to be your guide by sharing what has worked to get me through my struggles and forward on my climb. I recommend you take each concept in this book and apply it as you see fit, adapted to your own beliefs, interests and talents.

Each of us is starting with a different background, level of experience and understanding, but anyone can apply the ideas in this book to Grow a Pair of Antlers or make them stronger. I will guide you through the planning and preparations for your climb, then take you each step of the way from the foothills to the summit to help you become a Fearless Doe and implement the skills required to Lead Your Herd. It does not matter if you are new to the work world or have years of experience, there is always room to learn and grow.

Perhaps you are just starting out on your career. Do you feel too young to lead? Or maybe you have an entry level position and title and can't imagine how that offers opportunities to lead? I understand how you feel. I began like you and worked my way up the corporate ladder. But it's important to understand that leadership is not a title. It is a set of applied values, attitudes, and strategies. Promotions and titles are given to people who are already leaders. A title grants you management responsibilities. It does not confer the respect earned by an influential leader. Management is important to an organization's productivity, but leadership has the power to change people's lives. In this book, I share the values and skills I used to strategically climb to a leadership role in my career so you can incorporate them into your journey to achieve your goals. For now, just start with where you are and what you have. A leader's influence is not limited by age, gender, race, education or title. You only need Intentional Purpose and Courageous Actions. This book will be your guide. Congratulations on your decision to take action, read this book, and pursue your goal to become a Fearless Doe!

Or, perhaps, you already are a manager or a CEO, but you want to make a bigger impact. You want to be a better leader. You are successfully managing day-to-day operations, but feel you could be inspiring and mentoring your staff to a bigger and better cause. This book is designed to help you connect with a deeper purpose. The world needs your commitment to sharing your message and passion with others. Perhaps you feel the responsibility of leaving the world in a better place than it was when you arrived, much like I do. You already understand a Fearless Doe's legacy is actualized in service to others, but you want to be more intentional and focused on this goal. This book describes the personal and relational techniques I used to increase my influence and make a bigger difference. You may be able to add some or all of them to your backpack as you continue on your journey. I respect you for taking the initiative and time to read this book to take your Influential Leadership to the next level. Take a moment to feel proud of the impact you have already made in people's lives and your desire to give even more!

Before we get started, here is a brief overview about how this book is organized. It is divided into two sections.

'Section One: Grow a Pair of Antlers' is the foundation for succeeding on the journey to leadership. In this section, I will discuss the values and attitudes you can adopt and exemplify on the path to the summit of influence. The guides at the end of each chapter will help you affirm your values and practice gratitude to prepare you for the climb ahead. In 'Section Two: The Fearless Climb', I explain the critical performance skills you can master to maximize your impact in the world. I have grouped these skills into the three key outcomes from your efforts: Intentional Purpose, Courageous Actions, and Influential Leadership. The worksheets at the end of these chapters will help you gain clarity, take bold action, and make determined progress. They will also prepare you for the opportunities and responsibilities of leadership.

Wherever you find yourself on the path of clarity and confidence in Leading Your Herd, your desire to be a Fearless Doe - to make a positive difference in the world - is an indicator of the amazing purpose and courage already within you. I congratulate you on your initiative to Grow a Pair of Antlers!

I encourage you to visit www.TheFearlessClimb.com for additional resources. You will also have the opportunity to connect with other Fearless Does who are on this journey with you. I look forward to getting to know you!

Introduction

Our deepest desire is to know our life has meaning. We crave to believe we were created for a higher purpose. That we were formed with loving attention to detail and great care. We want to feel beautiful, precious, and loved, even with the imperfections stamped on us by our past. We desire loving kindness for our fears and grace for our mistakes. We hope that our struggles have meaning and our contributions make an impact in the world. We want our legacy to have eternal value.

We also want to accept and embrace who we are so we can confidently use our talents to share our wisdom and love with those around us. We know we have so much encouragement and joy to give, but our perspective shifts during our hectic days and anxious nights. We forget - or just don't have the energy or confidence - to live our lives to their fullest potential. If you relate to some or all of this message, you are not alone.

Most of us struggle with the pressure to appear perfect and happy while hiding feelings of inadequacy and loneliness; with the guilt of losing our patience at home, of showing our emotions at work, of envying our friend's vacation photos. All these feelings secretly and persistently erode our happiness. Everyone else seems to have their act together in their social media posts and we wonder what's wrong with us. As a result, we are terrified to share our insecurities with anyone. We don't want to be judged or considered weak. We "have to be" strong for everyone who depends on us - our spouse, our kids, our parents, our friends, and coworkers.

We ask ourselves, 'Why are we unhappy when are blessed with - or lucky to have - so much stuff and opportunity?' We are told we can be anything we want to be and have anything we want to have. On the surface, it is an empowering message, but in reality, it is exhausting. We realize we can be anything, but not everything to everyone. We can have everything, but at the cost of our relationships and health. It feels like we are working so hard, yet still disappointing someone all the time. So we put our needs and dreams on hold for a day to just stay on top of all the demands. The days turn into months and years and we begin to lose our vibrancy. Do you feel trapped in a cycle of unfulfilling work and a hectic lifestyle? Do you feel like you have so much more to give than the mundane tasks you feel required to complete each day? Do you feel blessed in so many ways, but also guilty you are still unsatisfied; craving more meaning and joy in each day?

I wrote this book because that's exactly how I felt. I wanted more freedom. Freedom to work on what I wanted, where I wanted, and when I wanted. I wanted the freedom to enjoy my family more; to rest and relax; to experience life to its fullest potential - on my own terms. I wanted to be more courageous and take a leap of faith to create the lifestyle I was dreaming about. I wrote this book to intentionally pursue my dreams and to inspire you to do the same.

I believe that, together, we can discover better ways to find balance and inspiration, direction and confidence. I believe that sharing our experiences and leaning on each other more will lift us higher, collectively. I believe women have a valuable perspective and powerful voice we are still learning to use. I believe men have an imperative role and tremendous opportunity to partner with us to redefine what home and business teamwork looks like. I think we have untapped potential to serve our families and co-workers in a more integrated, efficient and powerful way. The benefits will include reduced stress and conflict and greater joy and success.

In our connected world, we have never-before-available opportunities to become leaders of love and integration in our families, our careers, our social groups, and in the media. Let's make it our goal to shift the discussions from blame and criticism to respect and community. Let's communicate, relate, and demonstrate a respect for each other in a way that's impossible for the world to ignore. Let's create a peaceful, but powerful, movement whose purpose is to overthrow old gender roles and race bigotries.

Let's create businesses where competent men and women are paid equally. Let's hire and vote for integrity, experience and knowledge, instead of judging a person by their race, gender, religion or bank account. Let's provide flexible work schedules to help families succeed. Let's share our dreams and aspirations with family and friends and ask for their help and support. Let's encourage each other while we juggle career, parenting, and eldercare responsibilities. Let's share our struggles and our success stories. Let's believe that our journey does not define us, it refines us. Let's embrace change and start creating the world we want to live in.

Let's also be honest and admit how difficult it is to publicly declare our mission. Standing up for the right thing is hard because we are countered by every demon of fear present in our minds. The fear of failure. The fear of rejection. The fear of pain. The fear of success. The fear of, well, everything in the future based on everything from our past. To counter these fears, we must remind ourselves only one place really exists. The present.

Only the present. That is all we have. This moment to love, to accept, to grieve, to comfort, to grow, to experience life to the full. God's love and grace is here. Right now. You are glorious. You are enough. Right now, just as you are. The art of leadership is to courageously believe this about yourself, then encourage each person you meet to believe it about his or herself.

You may not believe you possess the education, talents, or skills to make a difference in the world. I know you can do it because I have personally witnessed passion, strength, and determination in many people who had every right to blame other people, or the circumstances of their life, or the state of the world as their excuse. People of all shapes, sizes, colors, backgrounds, sexual preferences, belief systems, and more. Each one beautiful and enough, just as they are. They could have remained comfortably in their pity party, but they didn't. They were courageously vulnerable which transformed them into confident leaders who authentically and boldly shared their message.

You can do this too. You already have everything you need inside you. In this book, I share stories of everyday courage to help you find the confidence you may have lost along the way. I describe the steps you need to take to manage change in your life and take control of your future. And once you have Grown Your Antlers and become a Fearless Doe, you will be equipped to Lead Your Herd with intention, courage, and influence.

I believe we can create a better world - one where each of us is valued equally. One where our collective abilities shine brighter as a whole. A world where we stand in a circle, not in a line of shame. Transformative leadership is found in linked arms and loving embraces.

"Grow a Pair of Antlers: The Fearless Climb to Lead Your Herd" is about living life with Intentional Purpose, Courageous Actions, and Influential Leadership. This book is dedicated to our journey together to develop these qualities in ourselves and each other.

My Antler Story

I was 18 years and 1 week old the first time I saw a lizard. I know my exact age because I had just been dropped off at a college dormitory in California by my mom who was already on her way back home to Ohio. I stepped out onto the patio to escape the crowd in my dorm room and saw a little dinosaur twitch on the wall next to my head. I screamed and my new roommates laughed at me. I didn't feel very brave at that moment, but many people told me it took a lot of courage to move across the country alone. I guess I didn't know I was supposed to be afraid of the world yet.

In my remaining early adult years, many things bigger than that lizard scared me. I struggled to pay my apartment rent, slept on a mattress on the floor during a roach infestation, ran out of gas on the freeway, freaked out during my first earthquake, and escaped the unwanted advances of a date. But wonderful things were also happening because I was pursuing growth and opportunities.

So, in my naivety, I did more things I didn't know I was supposed to be afraid of. I applied for - and was hired into - an accounting job for which I had no previous experience or qualifications. I worked long hours to pay my way through college. I pushed through twelve years of evening and weekend classes to earn my bachelor's degree in business finance. I worked my way up the corporate ladder, and then left to create my own accounting consulting business. I worked on my business part-time while raising two kids and assisting elderly family members. And then I wrote this book.

I've discovered that courage is obvious in great feats of heroism, but it's undervalued and under-celebrated in the daily grind. If you attempt a little act of courage each day, you will be amazed at how fast this adds up to build your self-esteem and produce success. Courage in the face of risk is necessary for achievement and leadership. Here's how you know you are facing healthy risk: you feel a little bit of fear *and* excitement while you are contemplating the possibility. Don't allow the fear to win. If the opportunity is right for you, go for it. Then pat yourself on the back for being courageous. If it doesn't work out, that's alright. Your act of courage was the accomplishment.

My life of little courageous adventures has been fun and has challenged me at every turn. I faced fears almost every day and grew stronger. My faith grew stronger too. I still feel afraid; but when I do, I have confidence in my ability to overcome it. I made a lot of mistakes along the way, but I apologized and fixed them the best I could. More importantly, I learned from them and they made me stronger. As I matured, I became more capable at juggling multiple deadlines and handling stress. I utilized my leadership and communication skills and developed a cohesive vision for my life. I gained clarity about what kind of person I wanted to be and how I could positively impact the world. I became more focused, read a lot of books, took continuing education classes and attended seminars, sought wise counsel and pursued new skills. Little courageous steps I took every day added up and provided me with opportunities to make a few bold leaps.

I have done my best to assemble the most important lessons I have learned through my journey and am excited to share them with you. My goal is to provide you with a foundation and tools you can use to take little steps towards successful leaps on your own courageous journey to become a Fearless Doe.

GROW A PAIR OF ANTLERS

'SECTION ONE: GROW A PAIR OF ANTLERS' is the foundation for succeeding on the journey to leadership. In this section, I will discuss the values and attitudes you can adopt and exemplify on the path to the summit of influence. The Guides at the end of each chapter will help you affirm your values and practice gratitude to prepare you for the climb ahead.

"Do what you feel in your heart to be right - for you'll be criticized anyway. You'll be damned if you do, and damned if you don't."

— Eleanor Roosevelt

CHAPTER 1

BASE CAMP: MAP YOUR VALUES

'CHAPTER 1: BASE CAMP: MAP YOUR VALUES' describes the values that will boost your strength as you climb to the summit of Fearless Leadership. They also magnify your influence in the world by increasing your credibility and engendering respect. The values are Freedom, Integrity, Wisdom, Fear, and Faith. The 'Affirmations' Guide at the end of the chapter will reinforce these values in your mind and heart and boost your confidence to express them in your own unique voice.

"The future belongs to those who believe in the beauty of their dreams."

— Eleanor Roosevelt

Freedom

Fearless Does are women who seek to conquer their fears and limitations to experience more freedom. They serve with integrity and earn respect and influence to inspire their herd more effectively. They value and pursue freedom above all other goals, but they understand freedom comes at a price. To become a Fearless Doe, you must embrace uncertainty and discard the comfort of security. You must be ready to risk the appearance of foolishness and failure for the exhilaration of the climb and the joy and wonder at the summit. You must be willing to disappoint some people to inspire others.

The reward is the opportunity to pursue your passions and live with purpose and meaning. Freedom opens the door to living authentically. To honestly express your feelings and pursue your goals. To be free, you must care less about what people think about you. You will not be able to please all the family and friends you love. You will have to risk their disapproval. When you post your ideas into the world, you will be judged. Just accept that as the small cost of helping the many who are desperate for your support and encouragement.

Freedom includes the ability to choose how you respond to criticism. To choose what your mind dwells on. To choose what news, education, and emotions you allow into your personal space. You must make a conscious effort to live with intentional purpose and take courageous actions. You must not fit in with the majority. If people are judging you, celebrate your big rack of antlers! You have found the path to making your impact on the world.

One of the reasons we keep our opinions and ideas quiet is to protect our ego, our self-esteem, our public image. I recently saw a social media post by an old friend whose son is transgender. She is supporting his decision and helping him establish a new life as a woman. I was blown away by the courage it must have taken him to make such a dramatic and controversial change in his life. And I was equally impressed by the devotion of his mother's love. I wanted to post a message of encouragement to both of them and hesitated. What if my conservative friends saw my post? What would they think of me? I was ashamed of my insecurities and fears, especially compared to the boldness of my friend and her son. So I sent the message. My small gesture sent some love into the world and they received it. If my other friends want to condemn me for it, that is for them to defend to the creator of love. It's not my problem. I learned an important lesson in courage and my antlers grew a little that day.

Another reason we limit our adventures is to protect our worldly possessions. We stay in jobs we hate to protect our big houses or investment accounts. We turn on security alarms to prevent other people from stealing our stuff. We are striving for some feeling of security and control. I'm not suggesting you leave your car unlocked and running in the parking lot. But to be truly free, we must be realistic about the limitations of security. Security is a temporary illusion designed to help us sleep at night. The market could crash, war could start, a natural disaster could hit, or we could take ill - at any time - without any warning or ability to prevent it or control it. I'm not saying this to be scary and I don't suggest we dwell on or worry about any of this.

I'm suggesting we do what we can to pacify our fears about the future, then evaluate the risks and rewards of actions we can take today. When you focus on the present, you become free to live your best life now and become more comfortable with uncertainty.

Freedom is risky. It takes courage to give up the convenience of security. When we are born, we have no freedom. We are completely dependent on others. As we mature, we struggle against our parents' rules that keep us confined. At some point, we must go into the world and fight for our independence with hard work, sacrifice, and perseverance. Freedom is the product of discomfort. Much of the success of our life is determined by how hard we fight for freedom - how hard we work for it - the leaps of faith we take to get it. Fearless Does lean into discomfort because it leads to growth. They fly in the face of uncertainty because it precedes achievement. And achievement creates confidence and influence.

You have three choices for your life. You can fight against something. You can fight for something. Or you can remain passively silent. Silence empowers the bullies and the haters. It's time for each one of us to stand for something and speak out! When you give yourself the gift of freedom to stand for something, you will unleash the power and momentum of intention, courage and influence. You will be on your way to changing the world and making it a better place for all of us to share.

Integrity

Integrity means acting with high standards of performance, consistently, regardless of whether or not anyone is watching you. People trust and respect you when you demonstrate integrity through honesty, reliability, hard work, and authenticity.

Integrity is the outward demonstration of your inner character. Everything we do, every choice we make, and every word we speak is a reflection of our integrity. In our formative years, our character is shaped by our parents and teachers and the media. As we grow older, we become responsible for our character traits. Telling lies and making excuses is exhausting. The results are guilt, shame, low self-esteem, and broken relationships. When you choose to set high standards of integrity for yourself, you change the course of your life. People begin to trust you and treat you with more respect. A commitment to honesty, reliability, hard work, and authenticity improves your self-confidence, simplifies your life, and brings you peace of mind.

When I sold my accounting consulting business years ago, I started my job search with my client list. I decided to look for an opportunity in a company that was stable, but had potential for growth. A place where my skills would be valued and I could make a big impact. But the most important quality I considered was the integrity of the business owner. He or she needed to demonstrate a high level of integrity in how they managed their money, their customers, and their employees. I had many wonderful clients I could have talked with, but one long-term client met all the criteria. I made him a proposal, we negotiated a little, then he hired me as his company's Controller. We have been a very successful team ever since because we share the same dedication to financial integrity and the same heart to "Be a Blessing" (his company motto) to those we serve. When his company received an income tax audit notice from the Internal Revenue Service (IRS), we had peace of mind because we had confidence in the fidelity of our accounting records. We met the auditor with a smile and a spirit of helpfulness. As a result of our honesty, the IRS had no findings and the company owed no taxes, penalties or interest. When you do things with integrity, you give and receive blessings.

As you can see, honesty has been critical to my success as an accounting professional. Business owners trust me with their check stock and credit card numbers and online banking logins. They are assuming the risk that I might steal from them. To make sure I never give them anything to worry about, I will not sign their name on a document or even take one of their pens home. I am also straightforward in my recommendations about how they can manage their business more profitably and be more compliant to tax and employment laws. Honesty means speaking the truth, respectfully and with love, even when it's uncomfortable for the receiver to hear or difficult for you to say.

Reliability is also important to my clients. They trust me to provide them with timely reports and ensure all their government filings are submitted on time. I keep my commitments to my clients, even if it means I am up early or late to complete an assignment or have to cancel a personal appointment to get it done. I haven't been perfectly reliable, but I rarely miss a deadline. As a result, my clients give me grace when I do have an unavoidable delay. And, because

I know I always do my best to keep my promises, it is easy for me to communicate any challenges I am having without hesitation or guilt. Reliability means keeping the promises you make to others.

Reliability and hard work are twin sisters of integrity. Oftentimes you just need to "suck it up" and just get it done. There are few shortcuts to accomplishing your goals. Some lucky people hit it big out of the gate, but most people show up day after day for years to build their business and create their wealth. They work hard and they don't give up. If you are acting lazy, don't expect to succeed at very much in life. Lazy is not who you are, it's a lifestyle you have adopted. You can choose to get off the couch and off your phone and get to work. The question is, would you rather be filled with purpose and make an impact in the world or watch another episode of reality television? Integrity is a choice - a choice to make the climb towards success.

Finally, integrity is about being authentic in relationships. Authenticity is similar to honesty, but more specifically means you are allowing your real personality, gifts, interests, passions, struggles, and quirks to shine through consistently with others. Sharing your story authentically has the magical power to connect you with people of all different backgrounds and interests because we still share the same human experience. We are all striving and hoping for something more, struggling with fears and illnesses or tragedy, and loving, laughing, and crying. When we talk about our shared experiences with humility, we can provide support and encouragement to each other. Authenticity is emotionally risky, but it is the pathway to love, acceptance, respect and trust.

Integrity is not one single behavior of a successful person; it is the combination of high standards, in multiple disciplines, over a consistent period of time. It is the decision to be honest, reliable, hardworking, and authentic in all areas of your life. It is a decision to be a person who wants to earn respect and trust from others. A Fearless Doe feels proud of herself for living a life of integrity.

Wisdom

Do you remember the old cartoon that showed a trouble-making cat in his decision-making process? He had a tiny cat image on each of his shoulders. One had little wings and a halo. The other had red horns and a long pointy tail. We understood, even as little kids, that the cat was making a choice between a good and bad idea. He had two thoughts and could control which path he took. His choice would determine the plot of the rest of the show.

You are like that cartoon cat. You also have two little "cats" on your shoulders. Your choice determines the plot of the rest of your life. The good "cat" represents love and compassion. It is the love and compassion you give yourself, then to others. The bad "cat" represents fear and judgement. This is the fear of failure and an unforgiving attitude towards yourself. When you choose to believe negative things about yourself, your relationships may be impacted through your defensiveness or passive-aggressive behavior. You may become embroiled in emotional arguments and blocked from creativity and productivity. You may feel unworthy of love which means you will find it difficult to give love.

Notice that love is the opposite of fear and compassion is

the opposite of judgement. If you are feeling love and compassion, you are choosing good thoughts. If you are feeling fear and judgement, you are choosing bad thoughts. Let me be clear, you are not a bad person, but your thoughts can be bad. Your thoughts are separate from you - they do not define who you are. We are, however, all tempted by bad thoughts. And, we are also all given the power to refuse them. You have the authority to argue with a thought, tell it off, command it to leave, or simply ignore it. In all cases, you can choose to replace a negative thought with a positive one. Your thoughts create your emotions and your motions. If you choose the good thoughts of love and compassion, your confidence will rise and your relationships will thrive. Your actions will be a reflection of your good attitude. You will have more energy and focus to achieve your dream goals and make a real difference in this world.

But each of us is fighting a battle within our mind. One moment we think, "I can change the world!" The next thought is, "Who am I to change the world?" The positive forces within us can, but won't, destroy the negative forces within us without our permission. We have free will to choose our path. We have forgotten the power we have over our thoughts, behaviors, actions and destiny. The negativity rushes in when we are distracted or passive. When we aren't focused on our greater mission. Isn't that how battles go? The enemy waits and lurks in the shadows until their victory will be easy, like when you are tired, busy, and challenged by life. That's when the doubts and fears creep in and take hold. Alcohol, drugs, illness, pain, negative media, and draining relationships also lower our resistance. To succeed, we must be diligent. We must actively invoke the powers available to us. These powers are called love, hope, grace, faith and community. Ask for help. Battles are never won alone.

Your awareness and recognition of the battle is the first step. The next step is to attack the pessimism living in your mind and heart. Create a passionate vision of your future. Courageously believe in yourself and overcome negative thoughts with faith and positivity. Believe in those around you too. Help them, encourage them. Support each other authentically and win the battle together. Our journey is not meant to be travelled alone. No one person has all the answers. We must authentically share our mistakes and our struggles. We must release guilt and fear and replace these emotions with love and grace.

All of this begins with the selection - your choice, in your control - of which thoughts you allow to influence your emotions and beliefs and actions. Unproductive thoughts turn fear into anxiety and other negative thinking patterns, such as self-doubt, jealousy, and condemnation. Productive thoughts result in feelings of love and compassion, create positive relationships, and promote self-confidence and energy.

While it is important to be able to effectively reframe our thoughts in a *current* situation, it may even be more powerful to reframe our thoughts about *previous* events. This means not seeing failure as a blow to our self-esteem, but as a learning opportunity. It's about not taking everything so personally. When our parents argue, it's about their unmet 'needs', not ours. When kids, bosses, or spouses bully us, it's about their insecurities, not ours. When women gossip, it's about their emptiness, not ours. When men fight, it's about their pride, not ours. Every person is self-absorbed, including us, if we are being honest with ourselves. Unfortunately, we can take others down with us on our voracious desire for acceptance, security, certainty, and control. It takes emotional maturity to override our natural instincts and emotional baggage.

People physically mature without any conscious effort, but emotional maturity requires work. Our caregivers, teachers, and coaches demonstrate and teach us appropriate social behaviors when we are young. But when we become adults, we become responsible for our own continuing development. Most people stop growing at this point and become entrenched in blaming others from their past for their current and future situations. However, an emotionally mature person takes responsibility for their own emotions and actions. They consider how other people are feeling and how their attitude and words affect them. They learn to let go of grievances and self-pity so they can support, encourage and lead others into deeper connection and greater works.

Sometimes this requires help from a professional counselor or therapist. Be proud of yourself for asking for assistance to learn new skills. Why do we feel bad about this? We are not ashamed when we pursue classes for intellectual development or training for physical strengthening. When I told my daughter that her dad and I had been going to marriage counseling for a while, but I had been too embarrassed to tell her sooner, she said, "Mom! You guys are being such a good role model for us - seeking help and working hard on your relationship. I'm proud of you both!" Her comments completely reframed my thoughts about therapy. They convinced me we need to remove the stigma of pursuing knowledge and tools which will free us from our old, instinctive, emotional reactions. We should feel excited and proud of our initiative to learn new skills that will enable us to engage more openly and deeply with others.

You can become the master of your thoughts. Wisdom is just a form of mind control. You can learn to focus on the present, accept the past, and anticipate a positive future. You can become wise and choose to give grace, love, and compassion to yourself and others so you can create meaningful connections in all your relationships.

Fear

People say our greatest fears are of public speaking and death, in that order. But these are not the only fears we face. We have a seemingly never-ending supply of things - real and imagined - to be afraid of. It only takes one rogue thought to trigger a feeling of fear. Fear provokes our body's natural fight, flight or freeze response. Our body prepares us to either face our foe and challenge him or to run away as fast as we can. When our foe is not clearly defined or we don't feel we have the option to fight it or flee it, our mind is left with a surge of adrenaline and energy without a muscle to flex. We become frozen with fear and begin to ruminate and dwell on our problem. We use our brain "muscle" to try to think our way out of our situation. If you are truly in a problem-solving mode, this is a good thing. If you are in a situation where you are having difficulty finding a solution and feel stuck, fear of the future can develop into anxiety. Anxiety can trap its victim in a cycle of anger, resentment, frustration, hopelessness and depression.

As a result, our potential to impact the world, serve others, and lead an amazing life can be thwarted by just one fearful thought. We can monitor our thoughts and guard our emotional energy by avoiding negative inputs, like political news that upsets us. We can also learn to redirect negative thoughts to focus on options and potentially positive outcomes. If change is in our control, we can take action. If not, we can choose to just move on with our lives. Sometimes we must simply accept a situation and not dwell on circumstances beyond our realm of influence.

One of my fears is claustrophobia. I am afraid of small, tight spaces. I do not explore caves and I avoid tunnels. But it's not always possible. My husband has season tickets to the NASCAR race at the California Speedway. While the track was being built - long before we were married - he bought two seats at the start-finish line and an RV spot in turn two. When we got engaged, I called this my signing bonus! We love going out to the races together. I enjoy the excitement and the sounds and the energy of the people and the engines. However, I don't enjoy the tunnel that goes under the track. We must walk through it to go from the stands where our seats are located to our RV spot in the infield. Sometimes, there are not many other people in the tunnel and we can walk through in a minute. Other times, the tunnel is packed with people and we are just shuffling through as a herd. It only takes a few more minutes to go through, but when I see the crowd, I feel anxiety rushing to the surface of my consciousness. I have developed a process to help me deal with those feelings.

First, I remind myself that I am in control of my feelings - they don't control me. Then, I assess if I am truly in imminent physical danger. (The answer in that short tunnel is always no.) My husband automatically takes my hand when we enter the tunnel, so I mentally acknowledge I have someone with me who can help if we get into trouble. Finally, I fix my gaze ahead at the light at the end of the tunnel above everyone's heads. By the time I have processed all this in my head, we are almost completely through anyway. I recommend the same steps for any non-life-threatening fear you are facing.

1. Affirm control over your feelings.
2. Assess the likeliness, imminence and potential negative repercussions.
3. Create or remind yourself of the plan for getting through the situation.
4. Ask for encouragement, support or help.
5. Look for the light at the end of tunnel.

Every time I see the crowded tunnel at the track, I have an involuntary reaction of fear. I can choose to stay in my seat and avoid the situation. Or, I can choose to go through it and manage my thoughts and feelings until I get to the other side. These are the types of choices we make every day and they determine the quality of your lifestyle and potential for a significant legacy. When you take control of your fearful thoughts and emotions, you can walk through uncomfortable situations and enjoy the rewards of living your life with purpose and courage.

Faith

I am a Christian. This means I believe Jesus Christ is the living son of God who came to earth and died to reconnect imperfect humans with our perfect father. I also believe he rose from the dead to prove to us our souls have eternal meaning and purpose beyond our brief time here on earth. Why do I state my faith to you in this book? Because it empowers me to believe I have a loving God on my side who will help me fight the battle against fear in my mind and I believe faith can do the same for you.

Hope gives me energy and enthusiasm to get up every morning to encourage and support other people as we share this adventure of life together. I don't pretend to have all the answers. I also want to make it clear I do not consider myself perfect. In fact, Christian faith is built on the heart-felt repentance of our mistakes and the acceptance of God's unconditional gift of love and grace. All faiths, Christianity is no exception, get distorted by self-aggrandizing politicians and religious leaders and other judgmental hypocrites. I encourage you to look past your cynicism caused by these twisters of truth and take some time to explore the original testimonies of Jesus' life, words, and values. If God exists, you will have spent your time in no better way. God promises if you seek him with an open heart, you will find him.

The New Testament of the Holy Bible describes in detail the life of Jesus Christ. You may know that his death on the cross (a common Roman form of execution at the time) was a propaganda ploy by power-hungry, religious leaders because Jesus was speaking out against their hypocrisy. He was angry those leaders were obfuscating religion for their personal gain and preventing people from enjoying an authentic relationship with God. Multiple eyewitness accounts describe how much Jesus loved and valued every person. He even called it the greatest command to love God and love each other.

Surprisingly, a story about Jesus' followers - his disciples - had the biggest influence on my belief in his story of death and resurrection. The people around Jesus were terrified when he was arrested prior to his execution. They denied knowing him, ran away, and hid in fear. I would have done the same. But the story takes an incredible twist. It says Jesus rose from his grave three days after he died. It states he visited with the disciples for forty days. He proved his identity to them by showing the holes in his hands and his feet where they had been pierced by the nails that pinned him to the cross. This all sounds absolutely crazy to me. But the next part of the story convinced me to take it seriously and consider the possibility that it was true. The disciples didn't hide anymore after Jesus ascended into Heaven. They courageously travelled to many countries to proclaim the good news of eternal life and were often imprisoned and/or executed as a result. They weren't afraid of death anymore! I don't know about you, but I would have stayed hidden in a locked room to avoid execution. I'm a little nervous to share my faith so boldly in this book and I don't even have to worry about imprisonment or death. I sincerely believe Jesus' followers personally witnessed life after death. I'm just asking you to consider the possibility of a God who loves you so much he would send his only son to give you a message of eternal meaning and hope.

I am sharing this with you because God says in the Bible he will leave the 99 sheep to find the lost one. You may be the lost sheep he finds today. He wants you to know He loves you and you are worthy.

God has given you free will to accept or reject His gifts of love and hope.

You can tell God you believe in Him and accept forgiveness through Christ right now.

If you would like more information, please go to my website at www.TheFearlessClimb.com/Hope.

'Affirmations' Guide

To prepare your heart and mind to believe you have power to succeed locked away inside of you, confidently declare the following affirmations. Hang a copy of this page on your bathroom mirror. Repeat these statements out loud to yourself every morning and evening for a daily boost of confidence. Try looking at your eyes in the mirror while you are speaking. It may feel uncomfortable at first, but you will experience more powerful results over time. Your heart and mind will begin to internalize this message and you will feel your antlers growing!

My past does not define who I am or
what I can accomplish today.
I receive grace for my past.

My life has meaning and purpose.
I am unconditionally loved.

I am free to create my authentic
lifestyle and my eternal legacy.
I take responsibility for my present
thoughts and actions.

Peace and joy are available to me right now.
I deserve to be happy.

I have faith in God and confidence in myself.
I have hope for my future.

I am Intentional, Courageous, and Influential.
I am a Fearless Doe!

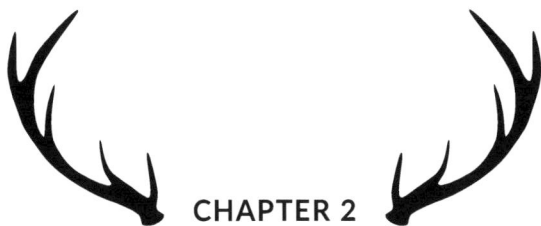

CHAPTER 2

BASE CAMP: PACK YOUR ATTITUDE

'CHAPTER 2: BASE CAMP: PACK YOUR ATTITUDE' describes the mindsets you can adopt to surmount challenges and make it to the summit of influence The attitudes are Humility, Creativity, Indomitable Will, Flexibility, and Resilience. The 'Gratitude' Guide at the end of the chapter will enhance your emotional stamina and help you appreciate the journey through all its ups and downs.

> *"People grow through experience if they*
> *meet life honestly and courageously.*
> *This is how character is built."*
>
> — *Eleanor Roosevelt*

Humility

I have always been a competitive person. I like this quality in me. Having the desire to win drives me to work hard, focus, and do my best, but sometimes it can get me into trouble. Many years ago, the company I was working for held a costume competition for Halloween. My girlfriend and I decided to dress up as a team and spent most of the night before making our costumes. We were a hamburger and french fries. She was the talented, creative energy behind the scenes. I was just a helper. We shopped, and cut, and sewed, and spray-painted, and produced top-quality work. We looked amazing! I would like to say we won the competition, but we didn't. When the votes were tallied, our co-workers voted for me as the french fries, not my friend as the hamburger. We hadn't thought to tell them to vote for us as a team. I was thrilled at my victory and didn't once mention my friend. I didn't thank her. I didn't state that we were a team. I just basked in my glory. It took a perceptive co-worker to pull me aside and remind me about her feelings. That win almost cost me my best friend, but it taught me an important lesson about humility.

I learned that humility is the attitude of appreciation that our accomplishments are a result of the support and talents of the people around us. Even if our success in a particular situation was a solo act, we must not forget all the people - parents, teachers, coaches, friends, and leaders - who taught us and believed in us. This does not mean that we are to minimize our role in the project, nor does it justify sacrificing our self-esteem or pride in a job well done. Humility is not about being a martyr with a victim mentality. It simply means you should keep your ego in check and share the credit with your team. Allow others to feel good about themselves as well. Rick Warren says it best in his book, "The Purpose Driven Life: What on Earth am I Here for?": "Humility is not thinking less of yourself; it is thinking of yourself less. Humility is thinking more of others."

Humility is also an awareness of your own imperfections so you do not become judgmental and hypocritical. It's believing we are all just doing the best we can at any time and respecting that we are all at different places in our journey. Humility is the act of accepting and giving grace. It is a heartfelt belief that God created each person exactly right. Perfect, before we were subject to the mistakes of our ancestors and of our own free will. Thankfully, God's grace picks us up and dusts us off again and again. Gratitude for those fresh starts produces humility in us. When we acknowledge that we all need grace, we work together with more patience, respect and camaraderie.

As a result, humility is the leadership attitude that helps create success. We win, but not at the expense of others. We lift others up with us. We win together as a team where no one is left behind. It's how a Fearless Doe leads her herd.

Creativity

When I was twelve years old, I entered a drawing contest for the chance at winning a $25 cash award from a "prestigious" art school advertising in a children's magazine. The challenge was to draw my favorite of three characters, between "Tippy" the turtle, "Tiny" the mouse, or a no-name pirate. I chose "Tiny" the mouse. I meticulously copied each line and shade in the little black-and-white sketch and mailed it in with my name, address, age, and telephone number. I eagerly awaited the response to my perfectly accurate rendition of their cute little rodent. Sadly, I never heard back from them. Several months later, they published one of the drawings that won a prize. It looked nothing like the image I copied. It was a talented young artist's creative rendition of "Tiny" with all sorts of extra lines and squiggles that were not in the original masterpiece. That was the moment I realized I was not artistically gifted. I was a logical, methodical person, not an artistic, creative one. The thought that I was not a creative being became part of my self-identity.

Twenty-five years later, I started my own consulting service. I was developing systems and brainstorming ideas and building my business. I was thinking outside the box and stretching my imagination and filling my mind with possibilities, then making them real. I was solving problems and juggling deadlines and managing people. I was startled to realize I was being very creative! I embraced it as my new self-image. I didn't change who I was, I just changed the way I thought about myself. It was an empowering attitude and it increased my confidence.

Creativity is the energy of life. It enables us to dream and then implement. To believe in something more than what we can hold in our hands today. It allows us to take disparate ideas and mesh them into something new and wonderful. It is inspiration and appreciation. The goal of creativity is freedom of personal expression, in any form. The medium we choose to express our ideas is irrelevant. To be creative is to remove the boundaries of what is accepted as known or plausible. You must try and fail and try again; imagine, stretch, and grow; seek and ask questions. You must be thankful for what is known, but believe in what is unseen. Creativity is an attitude of positivity. It is the canvas on which you can paint the future.

Here is a list of some ways I inspire myself into creative thinking:
- I visit an art museum.
- I listen to music.
- I hike a local trail.
- I go on a walk and listen to the birds or stare at the stars.
- I breathe deeply and meditate.
- I read a funny travel book.
- I watch online videos of hip-hop dancers. (Yes, you read that right!)

You will have your own list of creative prompts, but the goal is to put yourself in a happy and inspired state of mind. Enjoy! Your possibilities are limitless!

Indomitable Will

As of the writing of this book, I have earned a purple belt in Goju Shin-Ryu Karate. Although I am still on my journey to black belt, I have supported my son and husband as they met their goals. As a result, we have a lifetime membership at our dojo, the American Martial Arts Academy in Southern California. At this family-friendly facility, people are promoted based on their personal best efforts and attitude, not on performing martial arts katas with perfect style. This builds confidence at any age, but is especially effective with children. To the parents reading this, I highly recommend martial arts in addition to other organized sports - for your sons and your daughters.

The Academy's approach to training enables people of all ages to succeed, regardless of physical challenges. For me in my 50's, this means I can't make my weak right hip, ache in my lower back, or fused discs in my neck, an excuse. I need to just do my best every time I am in the dojo, so I bring a positive attitude, a determined focus, and my best effort.

Karate is obviously a physical activity. But surprisingly, it also requires a lot of mental stamina. It is the integration of acute awareness, quick reflexes, and the strategic use of energy. To get promoted past the first few belt ranks, you must also have determination. The kind that is unwavering in its resolve - it must be resolute. A resolute person is admirably purposeful, determined, and unwavering. Our karate oath uses a similar, but more powerful word for determination: indomitable. Its literal meaning is to be impossible to subdue or defeat. An indomitable will in karate refers to both physical prowess in the moment and the determination to finish the journey, even through adversity over the long haul. Notice I said the determination to finish, not the determination to win.

During training, I am often sparring against men who are bigger, taller, and stronger. They are competitive and intimidating. We have rules against intentionally hurting each other, but if I walk into a punch or don't keep my hands in front of my face - well now, whose fault is it if I get clocked in the nose? It happened once and the entire group watching went silent for a moment - waiting to see my reaction. I remember feeling...how? Proud? Exhilarated? Challenged! I quickly said I was fine, put my hands back up, and went full-on back into the ring with a huge smile on my face. I didn't score even one point against my opponent, but I finished the match with enthusiasm. I lost the competition in the dojo, but won the battle inside me. That day infused me with courage and a physical and mental confidence I carry with me today. (And in case you were wondering, my nose is fine!)

You will often be challenged this way in life. The project you are tackling, the new business you are starting, the relationship you are developing will feel big and intimidating. But you must have an indomitable will. Don't give up, just keep on working. Don't try to win, just finish. Don't try to be perfect, just get to completion. If you do this enough times, you will eventually hit your goal. And above all, smile through it. Life is an adventure. Live it like you are on a roller coaster and feel the thrill. We are always worrying about what others will think about us. Do they think we are full of crazy ideas? Pursuing foolish goals? It doesn't matter what they think. You are the one who has to look back at your life and consider if you lived it fully. Your confidence, courage, and wisdom grow every time you take a punch. Put your hands back up and go full-on back into it with a huge smile. Ultimately, people will express amazement and wonder at the joy of your adventurous spirit and strength of your indomitable will. They will recognize you as a Fearless Doe.

Flexibility

My grandma, amazingly, could play music by ear. She was able to hear a song and immediately play it on the piano, organ or accordion. Grandma Betty was a prodigy who entertained audiences for almost 90 years. She was mentally alert her entire life, but became wheelchair bound and physically dependent in her final years. She had suffered from arthritis for as long as I could remember and it had finally overtaken her. Her hands were knotted and constricted and she slumped over to one side of her chair. Her disability eventually ended her career. She was always in pain, but tried not to complain about it too much because she appreciated our visits. I didn't understand how much she must have suffered until I had neck vertebrae fusion surgery.

My surgery went well. It resolved the acute nerve pain I had been experiencing. However, I continued to have painful muscle spasms in my shoulder that would occasionally keep me from work or from enjoying my family. I was determined to resolve my physical issues and set out to try various options. The most beneficial remedies provided me with flexibility. My regimen became yoga every morning, walking every evening, reformer Pilates once a week, and a massage and chiropractic adjustment every other week. Does that sound like a lot? It is! I didn't think I had the time for any of it, but I soon discovered I had even less time for suffering in misery and pain. I realized if I didn't maintain physical flexibility, I couldn't live my life with joy or service to others. The pain would drain my power to succeed.

Physical flexibility is only one kind of flexibility necessary for success. Another form of flexibility is the balancing force to indomitable will. It is mental flexibility. This is the opposite of stubbornness. When you make a decision and establish a plan, you are setting actions into motion based on the available information and circumstances of that moment in time. You can set goals and make commitments, but you need to remain flexible about how to achieve them.

I started my accounting business before cloud internet

services were mature and prolific. When I signed clients up for monthly services, I committed to visit their office once a month to complete reconciliations and other consulting work. Many years later, I decided to transition my business model to remote services utilizing a cloud hosting program and remote access technologies. I asked my existing clients to be flexible and supportive of my new procedures. I would do the same work from my office instead of theirs. The technologies simply did not exist when I made the commitment to visit them in person every month. They were flexible enough to agree to the new process.

You also might need to be flexible about whether or not to continue to pursue a goal you set. After twelve years, I decided to sell my company. I had taken it as far as I wanted to. I didn't start the business with plans to close it, but I was flexible enough to notice when it was time to move on.

The final type of flexibility is useful in solving problems or while making decisions as a partnership or team. I do not have all the best ideas. I might like to think I do, but I don't. No one does. That's why it is beneficial to strategize with other people when determining a plan of action. This could be your spouse, your team at work, a coach, or even your child. When they have the opportunity to bring ideas to the table - and you thoughtfully consider and discuss them - they feel valued and will give more support and take more ownership in the outcome. In addition, you will likely arrive at a better solution or plan than you would have alone. I like to think of it this way: disclose, discuss, decide. First, disclose the problem up for discussion. Then, ask for the other person's opinions and ideas. Ask them clarifying questions. After they have shared their thoughts, it's your turn to talk about your ideas. Finally, make the decision. If there is a boss or parent in the meeting, they get to make the final choice. If there are equal partners in the room, the one who identified the problem and started the conversation gets to make the final decision. With this rule, the more proactive person gets more control. Passivity does not get rewarded.

Set goals and make decisions, but get input and listen to others' ideas, and be flexible with the approach and commitment as you receive new information or the situation changes. Flexibility is a critical component to unlocking your creativity and momentum to succeed. Some people will accuse you of changing your mind with a negative tone in their voice. You may be tempted to feel bad about this. Don't. This is the prerogative, or more accurately, the imperative - of a high-performing individual. To live to our fullest potential, we need to dream and plan. As we take action to pursue our goals, God will put new people, opportunities, and information in front of us we could not have anticipated. Part of living in faith is to expect and watch for His divine guidance. Then, with wisdom and prudence, adjust course and step out with trust. With that in mind, may we never feel like apologizing for changing our minds or being flexible ever again.

Resilience

Resilience is the ability to recover emotionally from a challenge, problem, or failure...to be able to learn from these experiences and believe they will make you stronger and can contribute to your future success.

Researchers at the University of Pennsylvania have identified several factors that affect your ability to bounce back from a setback. Most of it has to do with your interpretation of the situation. Some of it has to do with the support systems you have in place. But the first factor is biological.

The first factor is how your body responds to stress. Some people get headaches, others have digestive problems. When we work too hard and forget to breathe, stretch, and take breaks, our bodies scream out with pain to tell us to relax. Our immune systems weaken and we might catch a flu bug. It can take an hour or two to recover from a busy week, or it can take days to feel better. All of that recovery time is lost. We don't feel well enough to enjoy our time off or to be productive. Physical health is critical to our ability to bounce back from adversity.

The next factors that affect your resilience are self-awareness and self-regulation. Some people are naturally more in touch with their feelings than others. But if you're not sure, you can ask yourself the following questions at any time. The first question is 'How do I feel right now? The second is, 'What can I do to improve my emotional state?' The more accurate you are in the description of your feelings and the more successful you are at managing your emotional state, the more likely you will be to adapt and overcome challenging circumstances.

Other factors include mental agility, mastery, and optimism. If you can look at problems in different ways, brainstorm some solutions, and believe in your ability to implement one of them and improve your situation in the future, you will be more resilient than someone who gives up because they have no hope.

The final factors in resilience are based on your relational connections with family, friends, and social institutions like the workplace or a church. Your belief in a higher purpose - something bigger than yourself - will also give you the strength to pick yourself up and brush yourself off.

Resilience is incredibly important in a leadership role. Your response to a mistake or a problem sets the example for the rest of the team. Your attitude can demoralize them further or fuel their fire to overcome the hurdle together. You can single-handedly, in one moment of reaction, create a cohesive bond within a team or break their spirit and cause conflict and disconnection. When something goes wrong, you need to bring a "can-do" attitude. Encourage everyone to pitch in and fix the situation. Ask for their ideas. Delegate the tasks. Keep everyone moving towards the solution. Blame does not have a place in this moment. You can discuss what went wrong later and provide some training or coaching. What everyone needs now is direction and action.

Practice the skill of resilience in your own life to keep making progress towards achieving your dreams. It will become a habit that will serve you well when leading and encouraging others to reach their goals as well.

'Gratitude' Guide

A regular gratitude practice helps to reduce stress and anxiety as it reminds us to appreciate the blessings we are already enjoying in our life. It keeps us present and humble and supports a more positive and healthy attitude.

Use gratitude to manage anxiety and build resilience:

1. Think of two worst-case scenarios related to the situation you are worried about. Take time to write down some ways to prevent the worst thing from happening or determine how you will manage the situation if it occurs.
2. Write down a few best-case scenarios.
   a. Connect them to vivid descriptions of powerful, positive emotions.
   b. Take several minutes to allow yourself to feel these positive emotions as if the best outcome already happened.
3. Create a purposeful action plan to create the best probable outcomes.
4. Express gratitude for this opportunity to learn and grow your antlers!

Daily gratitude practices:

1. Take turns at the family dinner to share your best and worst part of the day. This builds connection and trust within family members and creates a reliable, proven support group which helps with confidence and resilience.
   a. Congratulate each other's victories and celebrate their joyful moments.
   b. Support and encourage each other through any challenges or disappointments.
2. Write three things you are grateful for in a private journal every night before bed.

SECTION TWO

THE FEARLESS CLIMB

In 'SECTION TWO: THE FEARLESS CLIMB', I explain the critical performance skills you can master to maximize your impact in the world. I have grouped these skills into the three key outcomes from your efforts: Intentional Purpose, Courageous Actions, and Influential Leadership. The worksheets at the end of these chapters will help you gain clarity, take bold action and make determined progress. They will also prepare you for the opportunities and responsibilities of leadership.

> *"The purpose of life is to live it, to taste experience to the utmost, to reach out eagerly and without fear for newer and richer experience."*
>
> — *Eleanor Roosevelt*

CHAPTER 3

THE FOOTHILLS: INTENTIONAL PURPOSE

'CHAPTER 3: THE FOOTHILLS: INTENTIONAL PURPOSE' will provide you with various ways to think about and define your contributions to this world. You will contemplate how you want to live, who you want to serve, and how you want to be remembered. The specific aspects of motivation reviewed are Responsibility, Connection, Purpose, Legacy, and Lifestyle. The 'Plan Your Mission' Worksheet at the end of the chapter will illustrate how to put your hopes and dreams on paper to find clarity in your plans and develop your mission statement.

"It takes as much energy to wish as it does to plan."

— Eleanor Roosevelt

Responsibility

There is a story in the Bible in the book of Genesis about a couple named Adam and Eve. You don't have to be a person of faith to learn the lessons from their story.

The story begins with God creating and placing a man and his wife in the middle of a perfect garden. In the garden are two magical trees - one called the tree of life, the other the tree of the knowledge of good and evil. God warned them not to eat the fruit from either of these trees. The couple freely enjoyed their time with each other and with God. Genesis 2:25 says, "Adam and his wife were both naked, and they felt no shame." Then an evil serpent, wanting to disrupt the innocence and purity of creation, tempted the woman with power. He lied and said God didn't want her to eat the fruit from the tree of knowledge because she would gain wisdom God was withholding from her. Her ego liked the idea of having control and power, so she ate the fruit. Then, perhaps out of guilt, Eve seduced Adam into also taking a bite. Immediately after their snack, their "eyes" were opened and they realized they were naked. They sewed together some leaves for modesty. When God popped in for a visit, they hid from him. When he asked why they were hiding, they told him they were naked. He asked, "Who told you that you were naked? Have you eaten from the tree that I commanded you not to eat from?" Busted! It's easy to assume God already knew they had done that. It reminds me of my mom asking me, "Did you eat all the chocolate candy?" when I had it all over my little face and hands. And what did I say to that question? "My brother made me do it!" And that's the way Adam reacted to God's question as well.

"The woman you put here with me - she gave me some fruit from the tree, and I ate it." He blamed Eve for giving him the fruit and even blamed God for giving him Eve! How did Eve defend herself? She blamed the serpent. God punished the serpent, and Eve, and Adam. Everyone in this story was culpable, even though no one would take responsibility.

This story illustrates how our ego is the source of irresponsibility. Pride whispers fears of unworthiness in our minds. It rationalizes the breaking of promises and rules to gain personal glory. It convinces its prey to avoid commitment to minimize the risk of disappointment or failure. The noisy fears of losing out or making a mistake drown out the quiet values of honesty, trust, respect and vulnerability in a moment of decision.

We carry responsibility for our thoughts and feelings about the past. Each of us has had an experience with at least one person who has wronged us, and maybe even damaged us. Many people choose to stoke the fires of resentment towards those who have hurt them. Others find a way to forgive and let the anger dissolve. Forgiving others does not mean excusing their behavior. You do not have to say what they did to you was right or acceptable. It just means you are going to actively work through lingering emotional pain, possibly with professional help, and get on with your life. The hurts of your past do not have to determine your future. You can use what you have learned through your experiences to provide powerful support to others who have lived through similar circumstances. Empathy is a strong component of influential leadership.

Sometimes the past is heavy with how we have hurt someone else. Regret and guilt can wear you down and dim your light in the world. If you have hurt someone (by the way, we all have), it's time to take responsibility for that as well. Perhaps you need to apologize, admit your mistake and accept the penalty. Most importantly, you must find it in your heart to forgive yourself. You are not the same person you were when you did that thing. You know better now - that's why you feel guilt and shame. You were going through difficult circumstances. You were in emotional pain at the time and acted out. Your heart was hard, but now it's not, and it hurts. Your heart can be healed with grace. You can love others and not be afraid. You can love yourself and believe you deserve it.

After my parents divorced in my junior year of high school, I was angry, but was too young to understand why. My heart became hard and I hurt people with my callousness. My attitude and actions added shame and guilt to my pain. The turning point was when I read the book, "Hinds' Feet on High Places" by Hannah Hurnard. The allegory is about a young lady named "Little Much-Afraid". I didn't relate to that name very much. A hard heart acknowledges no fear. But, through the story, I received the powerful message of God's love for the person he created me to be. I believe he sees us as perfect and beautiful without all our mistakes disfiguring who we really are. I accepted grace for my mistakes and pardoned others for theirs. I now consider my past to have been a necessary part of my journey to become who I am today. I took responsibility for my present and my future by finding a way out of my past instead of allowing it to drag me down.

Responsibility is about demonstrating a stronger commitment to your personal integrity and important relationships than to your fears and insecurities. We can choose to listen to the snake or to listen to our hearts. Responsible people are self-confident and do not deny their actions or become defensive. Instead, they acknowledge their actions and accept the consequences. They also do not redirect blame to other people. If they make a mistake, they admit it, repent, and try to fix any repercussions. When you take responsibility for the direction of your life and the quality of your relationships, your ability to succeed and lead others improves exponentially. It takes courage to accept consequences and humility to admit mistakes. A Fearless Doe takes responsibility for her actions and her words.

Connection

One day when I was bored and flipping through channels on the television, I settled on a film of three people talking about connectivity while strolling around a beautiful, medieval monastery. It was the Le Mont Saint-Michel built upon an island off the coast of Normandy, France. The castle is only accessible at low tide, so it had been a fortress for hundreds of years. The movie is called "Mindwalk", based on a book by Fritjof Capra called "The Turning Point." This movie introduced me to the idea that we are all connected at the subatomic level to each other and everything around us.

In the 1930s, Albert Einstein and several of his colleagues observed a phenomenon of connectivity they called quantum entanglement. Basically, when any two atoms come into contact with each other, they experience an "unconditional bond" and have a direct influence on each other. George Boole, the creator of Boolean Logic, expanded on this concept and suggested that the world is one connected whole, but we observe it in parts. In fact, we are actually composed almost entirely of empty space. The nucleus of our cells is incredibly tiny compared to the size of the atom itself. We appear to be solid, but we are not actually touching a separate being when we hold hands or sit down. We are just experiencing the electromagnetic forces of the atoms interacting with each other. We are naturally, physically interconnected with everything in the universe. What requires unnatural effort is emotional connection.

Urbanization and our busy lifestyles have reduced opportunities to connect emotionally. Loneliness has become a modern epidemic. The antidote is authenticity and honesty with each other about our feelings and our need for help. We can't support each other if we aren't sharing our struggles and taking the time to listen and assist. We must be intentional about creating emotional connection with those around us.

I recently asked my dad about his childhood and went on a hometown trip with my mom. He grew up on an Ohio farm during the depression. She was raised in a small town in Indiana. Both were isolated from the world and lived with limited means and opportunities. They spoke nostalgically about the closeness of their families - geographically and socially. They were matter-of-fact about relationship dysfunction as if it was just ordinary and common. But they also experienced love and security through close support and connection among their relatives. My dad's extended family owned several small farms within walking distance of each other and shared food and child-rearing responsibilities. My mom's family also lived close together and was fiercely loyal and protective of each other. Her grandparents bought sixteen burial plots in the local cemetery because no one in the family ever left town. As the suburbs and middle class grew, so did the opportunities. During my childhood, men were walking on the moon and women were pursuing careers. Close family units were disbursing around the world.

Taking those trips down memory lane with my parents was bittersweet for me. It reminded me that freedom comes with a price. Globalization has broken the connection to our ancestors. Stress and loneliness are modern dysfunctions. For our emotional survival, we desperately need to break through our fake smiles, polite lies, and walled hearts. Connection is bonded through shared struggles and support.

Positive thinking, faith, and optimism are great tools for overcoming our fears and pursuing our goals. However, we may have taken this too far. It has become almost taboo to show our feelings of grief, depression, or loneliness. But we shouldn't feel afraid or embarrassed to share our real, natural emotions and ask for help. Let's choose to believe the best in each other and have hope in our future, but still allow ourselves to experience raw human emotions. Let's give permission to each other to be real and connect.

Purpose

Do you ever feel like God had so much more planned for you than you are experiencing? Sometimes you stare at your ceiling and wonder what's the point. Maybe you look off into the distance at the beauty of the sunset and crashing waves and wonder where you fit into the universe. Sometimes you feel so big and so important. Yet other times, so small and insignificant. You may be struggling to find your purpose. A clearly stated purpose defines who you want to help, inspire, lead, and influence. It describes the goals you want to achieve and how you want to use your resources of time, energy and money in their pursuit. Clarity in your purpose will help you make decisions about which projects to work on, what jobs to take, who you connect with, and how you accomplish all of it. Purpose allows you to confidently take your rightful place in the world and find meaning and joy in your journey.

Three months before beginning to write this book, I had no clarity about my purpose. I was grateful for a wonderful family and the security of a good job. I had taken a few chances in my life, developed a solid career, and loved and served others, but I had hit a wall. I felt like I was on a treadmill of life. I hesitated to make a change because I had the perceived security of a comfortable retirement in my future. I was over 50 years old and had a good job, serving with and for good people. My internal dialogue was resisting the idea of risking my conservative retirement plan. My fears kept reminding me it was time to hunker down and protect my assets and my energy. I felt old. Why? Because youth is about growing and learning. It's about living life with passion and fun and adventure. I was not living that way anymore. I had given in to the tiredness of the daily busy work and worries about the future.

Then it occurred to me that life goes in phases. The first 20 or so years of my life was spent on growing up and getting a formal education. I spent the next 30 years building my career and raising my family. God willing, I still have another 40 or 50 years left to live a new chapter and enjoy new challenges and experiences! Why was I giving up already?

I started writing in an 'Intention Journal' every morning. I wrote down all my crazy ideas and dreams. I did this every day. I also looked for images that represented what I wanted and saved them on my phone and looked at them every day. I started to see a pattern in how much money I wanted to make and where I wanted to live and who I wanted to serve.

After a couple of months of this, I did an internet search for "how to get off the treadmill of life" and found a video blog by someone named Brett A. Blair. I explored his website, completed his questionnaire, and signed up for a free consultation. I hired him to be my High-Performance Coach and talked with him every month. He sent me life-analysis worksheets and recommended books and held me accountable to my goals. In addition, he was a constant source of encouragement and wise counsel. My confidence in my dreams increased and my productivity sky-rocketed. I published this book one year from the day I started journaling. I had developed clarity about my purpose and regained my excitement for life. And, it led to a plan of action I was able to implement. You can do the same to become a stronger and more Fearless Doe with renewed passion and purpose for your life.

Legacy

Legacy is the memory of your purpose that lives on in others beyond your last breath. Creating your legacy is a bit like time travelling. You must use the urgency of your purpose to break free from your past, make bold decisions in the present, and take responsibility for the future.

Your past may have created some lingering impressions and feelings which are having a negative influence on your present attitude and actions. When you think about the past, you may dwell on feelings of shame, guilt, and anger which manifest as low self-esteem. However, your past does not have to define who you are in the present or determine where you will be in the future. You can choose to allow grace and forgiveness to reframe the past, heal your heart in the present, and clear your mind for the future. The future is an imaginary world created by your brain. When you think about the future, you can create feelings of anxiety and worry or of excitement and anticipation. You can either dilute your future with fear and passivity or season it with hope and determination. The present is where you make these decisions to define your past and your future. It's the place where your thoughts create your reality. To be healthy, confident, and successful, you need to accept grace for your past, take responsibility for your thoughts in the present, and embrace hope for your future.

The present is where we can experience an almost unexplainable peace and joy. We can get into the flow of creation and adventure in the moment and lose track of time. The past becomes irrelevant and the future takes care of itself. Lack of direction, purpose, and intention for our life produces idleness, passivity, and negativity in our mind. That's when we begin to dwell on the past and the future. We lose sleep. We are grumpy at work. We argue with our family. We wonder why our relationships are strained and our energy is depleted. The solution is to gain clarity about your desired legacy. Reconnect with what's important - with the priorities and purpose of your life. Then take action! Your passion for living will rebound and your joy will be contagious.

It's not automatic for us to consciously think about the legacy we are producing from our choices, but we are all creating it every day, even if passively. You can find it in our priorities, the decisions we make, and the way we treat other people. Someone who encourages and helps others is creating a legacy of love and service in their relationships. Another person may be creating a legacy focused on productivity and achievement. Their legacy is one of improving the world through accomplishment. However, someone who is careless with the well-being of others or obstructs progress may be attempting to protect their own self-esteem. They use the tools of defensiveness, blame, and redirection to protect the walls around their heart. These games produce whirlpools of conversation that drain time and energy from a team and block productivity on the important work; and consequently, respect and positive influence with others. A Fearless Doe establishes a vision for her legacy and actively connects to it her purpose. She then pursues it every day, in every interaction. It takes intention, courage, and influence to create the lifestyle you want to enjoy now while establishing the legacy you want to leave behind.

A useful (but a bit morbid) way to define your legacy goal is to imagine what you want people to say or think about you at your memorial service. How do you want them to feel when they remember you? Your answer to those questions is your legacy. It is the influence you had on other people during your lifetime. When you define your legacy, think about who you want to encourage and support. Your family and friends will probably be first on your list. That's a great start. Now think bigger. Think beyond your circle of acquaintances. We live in the most incredible time of connectivity in human existence. We are able to communicate with and impact people anywhere in the world, at any time. Technology has gifted us with the amazing opportunity to create a legacy with massive implications for love, hope, grace, respect, joy, and encouragement. When your definition of success is measured by the positive influence you had on another person's life instead of on your fame and fortune, you become present in the moment and focused on your mission in life.

What do you stand for? What's your legacy? Here is a formula to help you think about the answers to those questions:

$$(\text{Nature} + \text{Nurture}) \times (\text{Attitude} + \text{Actions}) = \text{Lifestyle}$$
$$\text{Lifestyle} \times \text{Influence} = \text{Legacy}$$

Your past is defined by both your nature and nurture. By nature, you were specially created with your own personality, gifts, and interests. Then, you were nurtured and uniquely shaped by your circumstances, experiences, and education. You can't change your past, but you can use it as a springboard to your success today and into the future.

Your attitude and actions in the present moment can transform your past - all your talents and experiences - into tools for creating your lifestyle today.

Multiply your lifestyle by your influential leadership to fulfill your purpose and produce a legacy that makes a difference in other people's lives.

Lifestyle

While legacy is focused on how you can love and lead other people, lifestyle is all about you. If you don't pursue goals you are excited about and gifted in, your sacrifice will become drudgery and your influence and impact will wane. You deserve to be happy and enjoy the lifestyle you desire for yourself and your family. Give yourself permission to think about what you want in life. What is your dream job? Your perfect relationship? Your ultimate vision of a balanced life?

Once you have created a vision for the lifestyle you desire, you can then think about how to make it become reality. We all have the same three types of resources available to us: time, money, and people. When we utilize these well, our lifestyle improves and our business becomes more profitable. The level of our impact and the success of our personal life or business venture is dependent on our ability to manage these resources. The key is to use all available resources efficiently and effectively. This requires intentional planning and effort.

When my daughter learned to drive and socialized more frequently with friends, we saw her a lot less. Even as a young adult, she lived at home, but didn't spend much time there. I was happy she was thriving and enjoying her life, but I missed having her around. I started thinking about ways for the family to stay connected with her. It occurred to me that she was spending a lot of money at restaurants. I thought if I improved my cooking skills, perhaps she would come home for dinner more often. The whole family would benefit from healthier, home-cooked meals and I would be learning some new skills. I watched celebrity chefs on TV, downloaded online recipes, and bought cookbooks. I started slicing and dicing and experimenting with fresh ingredients and flavor combinations. I had some flops, but I also created many successful dishes. I now plan the week's dinners in advance and add them to our family calendar so she can see them. As a result, she often comes home in time to eat dinner with us and we are able to catch up on the things going on in our lives. Connection with my family is important to me, so I sought out resources and invested my time and energy into creating opportunities for it to happen.

To consider your options and create a vision for your future, complete the 'Plan Your Mission' worksheet at the end of this chapter. It will be your guide on the path to achieving the goals for your purpose, legacy, and lifestyle. Repeat this process periodically because your mission statement will change as you learn and grow and transition through the various phases of your life.

Here is my mission statement as an example for you:

My mission is to boldly share my wisdom to inspire, teach, and guide others in their Fearless Climb to become Intentional, Courageous, and Influential Leaders.

I want to help people love God, love themselves, and love each other by embracing hope, grace, and the beauty of diversity.

Turn the page for a worksheet to help you create you own mission statement.

'Plan Your Mission' Worksheet

1. Write the vision for your Lifestyle here. Describe your perfect life. What do you want in your life? What are you working on? Who are you with? Where do you live? What do you enjoy doing in your free time? How much money do you have? What do you wish you spent more time on? Less time on? Anything else?

_____

_____

_____

_____

_____

_____

2. Write your Purpose and Legacy here. Describe the perfect world. What problems do you wish were solved? How do you wish people worked together or treated each other? What aggravates or upsets you? What do you want people to say about you at your funeral? When you are 90-years-old and looking back on your life, what will you have considered a life well-lived? Anything else?

_____

_____

_____

_____

_____

_____

3. Write your Abilities here. Describe the perfect job. What gifts were you born with? What talents have you developed? What skills have you mastered? What new opportunities interest you? What are you doing when you lose track of time? What education or experience might help you succeed? What do you love to do? Anything else?

_____

_____

_____

_____

_____

_____

4. Create your mission statement. On a separate piece of paper, write a quick draft of a few sentences based on the thoughts you shared above. Keep rewriting it until you have something that feels like it captures the essence of who you are and what you want, then write that version in the space below.

_____

_____

_____

_____

_____

_____

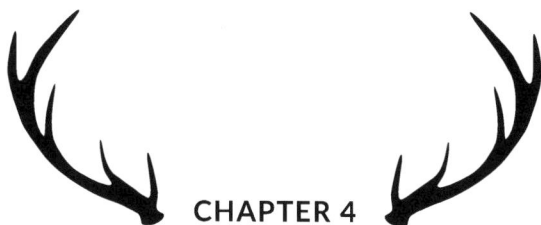

THE CLIMB: COURAGEOUS ACTIONS

'CHAPTER 4: THE CLIMB: COURAGEOUS ACTIONS' describes how small bold steps create momentum towards accomplishing your goals. I also discuss the attitude of a proactive leader to develop the courage to take the first step. The specific elements of fearless leadership I will review are Optimism, Confidence, Decisiveness, Courage, and Execution. The 'Take Bold Steps' Worksheet at the end of the chapter will encourage you to think creatively and connect action to your ideas.

"You must do the things you think you cannot do."

— *Eleanor Roosevelt*

Optimism

Optimism is sometimes described as an irrational belief in an unlikely positive outcome of events. A pessimist might suggest that the optimist should be more realistic. To the pessimist, a more realistic point of view might be to focus more on the likeliness of the negative outcome of events. In some circumstances, like in preparing for a natural disaster, this may be a good approach. However, neither optimism or pessimism accurately reflect our true circumstances. The element that is missing is our ability to influence the outcome. We are not merely playing a game of chance by choosing optimism or pessimism. We are placing a bet on our abilities. In addition, there is support from the scientific community and life experience that adopting an optimistic point of view will provide you with a healthier, happier, and more successful life.

Optimism fuels creativity by helping us keep an open mind to possibilities. It helps us take action and be productive. An optimist doesn't deny problems and setbacks, she addresses them. She acknowledges the world is uncertain and full of gray areas - that no decision is guaranteed to succeed or is final. This understanding allows her to make decisions, take action, review the results, and pivot until she reaches a successful conclusion. Optimism is related to hope and faith - all of which are founded in a belief in a brighter future. Optimism reduces negative thinking, anxiety, and worry. It enables us to visualize and attract the things we want more of in our lives. It may even help us live longer.

Pessimism is a depressing way to view the world. It lacks hope and vision for the future. A pessimist is more likely to give up, often before even getting started. When you choose pessimism and worry, you are stacking the odds against your success. You will be less likely to take the positive actions required to produce good outcomes. You will be imagining, ruminating, and attracting the things you don't want to have in your life. As her way to avoid risk of perceived failure and humiliation, the pessimist only addresses the negative and won't consider the positive. Fear convinces her that a positive outcome could not possibly happen - that she will never succeed and cannot feel happy, loved, and fulfilled. Fear is playing an evil trick on her mind but she can choose not to believe it. She can take a chance. She can make a decision and take action despite the fear. That's courage! And courage builds confidence and fuels optimism.

I have been to Las Vegas about a dozen times. I live in Southern California, so the drive is a little over four hours, which makes it a nice weekend getaway. I rarely gamble, but I do enjoy a quick trip with a fancy hotel, great food, and an incredible live show. The people and activity both fascinate me and wear me out. The slots bore me. The table games intimidate me. I drink in moderation and am uncomfortable with the blatant images and ads for strip shows. I try to like it. I think I should like it more than I do. But I can't talk myself into it. I look forward to going, but am fine leaving. Many years ago, my husband, Ed, took me to Vegas for a couple of days as an anniversary present. He had planned a nice dinner and show for the evening, so we dressed up to go out. We had some extra time before dinner, so he suggested I try a table game. I chose Texas Hold 'em poker because I had been watching the "World Series of Poker" tournaments on television and had picked up on some of the strategies. Ed and I had played each other a few times at home and I had beaten him handily enough to make him mad. If I had a chance of winning any game in Vegas, this was the one. He bought us some chips at the counter and the host sat us at different tables. I was shaking as I anteed up and was dealt my first hand. Then came the flop and a bet; the turn; then a bet; the river...oh my gosh! I have a great hand. My first time ever sitting at a table in Vegas and my hand is great! I go "All In", which means I bet all my money on that one hand. I'm shaking more now with the added excitement of big risk. I'm spinning in my own emotion and have no idea what anyone around me is doing or saying. I was obviously a rookie, so they bet on my ignorance and added their chips to the pot. I won it all! I heard a lady at the end of the table say something nasty about me and storm off. I usually want people to like me, but this time, I didn't care very much. I played a couple more hands conservatively. Ed busted out on his table and checked in on me. When he saw my pile of chips, he brought a couple of trays over to carry them away. I cashed out hundreds of dollars richer.

Why did I sit down to try table poker in Vegas at all, even though it scared me? The odds were not in the favor of a rookie winning any money against a full table of experienced players. Texas Hold 'em poker requires both luck in getting dealt good cards but it also requires skill to know when to bet and when to fold. The strategies of the bluff are not easy to pull off successfully. So why would I do it? Because I chose to be optimistic. I wasn't betting on the odds. I was betting on my abilities. I had confidence I could succeed against all odds. I placed a value on my skills and took a chance. That's courage. Not courage like a firefighter rescuing a puppy in a burning building, but a tiny amount of personal courage that developed confidence in my ability to take another risk at another time. You can't succeed at anything if you are unwilling to take calculated risks on yourself. You must keep trying. Develop a skill, then take a chance. It is the courage to try that builds self-confidence. You don't need to focus on the win or the loss. Only focus on the trying to build your optimism muscle and your confidence.

Confidence

Confidence is like a three-legged stool. You need all three legs for it to stand with strength and stability on the floor without wobbling or crashing down. The three legs of confidence are: accepting encouragement from others, attempting new experiences, and learning or developing skills.

The first leg of confidence is built when other people tell you, "You can do it!" You may have heard this message from a parent, teacher, or coach when you were younger. Later, you might have heard it from a spouse, friend or boss. Their encouragement may have prompted you to try something new, work a little harder, or improve an existing skill.

The second leg of confidence is built through experience. If you succeed at your attempt, you learn that you can try new things and have a positive outcome. You will be more likely to repeat something similar without any prompting from another person. If you are not very successful in your attempt, you learn that failure is not really that bad and you will have less fear and hesitation to try again. If the failure had repercussions, you handled and resolved them. Either way, you learned valuable lessons about what went right or wrong to apply next time.

The third leg of confidence is built by developing the wisdom and knowledge necessary to prevent problems and tackle challenges in the future. Perhaps you read books, attend classes, take an online course, or hire a coach to become more adept and gain more mastery. You develop foresight, planning, and leadership skills.

All three legs - accepting encouragement from others, attempting new experiences, and learning or developing skills - work together to build your confidence. For example, if you take a class in public speaking, you may have more courage to join a speech club where you will receive constructive criticism that will help you improve your skills and where you will experience people telling you, "You can do it!" It won't take long for your confidence in your public speaking skills to soar. Even better, when you increase your confidence in one area of your life, your overall self-esteem improves. You will have more courage to try or learn any new thing.

Confidence is built by taking action in the present. Taking action requires courage. Courage is a product of positive thoughts about the future. Positive thoughts can be cultivated from experiences in your past.

If you are faced with a scary challenge or opportunity you want to pursue, here is a confidence-building exercise for you to try:

1. Think of one of the following memories that is closest in nature to your current scary challenge or opportunity:
   a. A time when you learned or created something new.

b. A time when you fixed a mistake or solved a problem.

c. A time you attempted a new experience or met a new person.

2. Consider all the skills and gifts you used in that situation. Perhaps you used your intellect, communication skills, empathy, education, experience, determination, physical strength, faith, leadership influence, or something else.

3. Determine which skills you will need to take that first small step towards your current scary challenge or opportunity. (Note: The first small step may be learning a skill needed to take the next small step.)

4. Believe you can take that small step based on your past experiences and current skills and gifts. You can either do it successfully, or you can solve any problems that arise from doing it. Either way, you can do it. And doing it will build your confidence to do the next small step.

5. If you are still having trouble believing you can do it, call your most encouraging friend or family member to tell you "you can do it!" If you don't have an encouraging person in your life right now, hire a high-performance coach to challenge and encourage you. Accountability eliminates many fears.

6. Attempt the small step.

7. Repeat the exercise, if needed, to take your next small step.

Please notice I am saying "attempted", not "succeeded at", a new experience. Confidence grows every time you attempt something - success or failure is irrelevant. Both results serve one purpose - to teach you new skills and give you more wisdom. Throw yourself into adventure and growth. It's exhilarating and liberating to be free from the fear of failure.

Decisiveness

Making a decision is an intentional act of control over your life. When you procrastinate, you are handing control over to fate. Ironically, when you don't think you have made a decision, you actually did - the worst one you can make. You have made the decision to be a passive victim of circumstances. Instead, take control. Set a course and steer your ship. If you leave it to fate, you will end up crashed on the rocks and blaming the currents for your tragedy. The currents are neither good nor bad. They did not wish you any ill will. If you crash, it is your fault. But you won't know it. If you were passive, you won't take responsibility for the problem after it occurs because you didn't take responsibility to prevent it. You must make a decision, then take action, to steer your life to success. Our actions, based on our decisions, create our destiny.

Often, we avoid making a decision out of fear. Or we make a decision just to pacify our fear. We may feel like we don't have a choice, that we are being forced into a decision. Try not to succumb to the emotions of anxiety or frustration during your decision-making process. Remind yourself you have a choice. Think of a few options, even if they are not perfect or pleasant. Limit your options to prevent becoming overwhelmed. Give yourself the freedom to change your mind later, whenever feasible. Analyze your options and stay in control.

To help you evaluate your opportunities and make a decision, I recommend you ask yourself a series of questions that will help you consider the costs, risks, and benefits. I have put them together in the two part Courageous Action Decision System (CADS) shown below.

In Part 1, you will write out your answers to The Decision Questions. There are no right or wrong answers and your answers will be specific to the situation you are in right now. You may want to retake the questionnaire at another time to find out if your answers are different.

In Part 2, you will review your answers from Part 1 to work your way through The Decision Tree. This is how you will decide if you want to take the Courageous Action or not. If you decide not to take action, your confidence will not suffer since you made a conscious, well-thought-out decision to decline the opportunity or wait. If you decide to take action, your confidence will grow because you controlled your fears and boosted your courage.

If your decision has the potential to impact a partner or team, I recommend you collaborate with them and complete the CADS together. The Courageous Action Decision System will boost your confidence in the decision. You and your team will have buy-in which will lead you to take faster action on opportunities when they present themselves.

Few options are perfect, so just make the best decision you can, with the information you have, and move on in faith. Being decisive will help to override your fears, fill you with more courage, guide your actions, and contribute to the overall success of your leadership journey.

The Courageous Action Decision System (CADS):
Part 1: The Decision Questions

What action am I deciding whether or not to take?

_____

_____

_____

_____

_____

What are the potential costs of this action? What other opportunities might I lose?

_____

_____

_____

_____

What can I do to minimize these costs and/or reduce the risk of incurring these costs?

_____

_____

_____

_____

What are the potential benefits I could receive by taking this action?

_____

_____

_____

_____

How do I feel when I think about taking this action?

_____

_____

_____

_____

Part 2: The Decision Tree

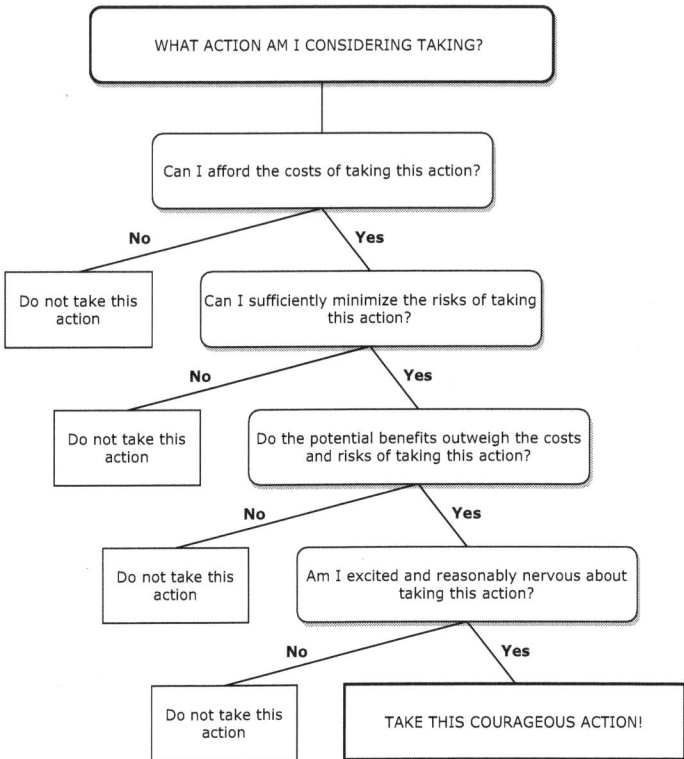

```
┌──────────────────────────────────────────────┐
│  WHAT ACTION AM I CONSIDERING TAKING?          │
└──────────────────────────────────────────────┘
                        │
        ┌───────────────────────────────────┐
        │ Can I afford the costs of taking    │
        │ this action?                        │
        └───────────────────────────────────┘
         No                         Yes
┌──────────────┐   ┌───────────────────────────────────┐
│ Do not take  │   │ Can I sufficiently minimize the     │
│ this action  │   │ risks of taking this action?        │
└──────────────┘   └───────────────────────────────────┘
                    No                        Yes
        ┌──────────────┐   ┌───────────────────────────────────┐
        │ Do not take  │   │ Do the potential benefits outweigh  │
        │ this action  │   │ the costs and risks of taking this  │
        └──────────────┘   │ action?                             │
                           └───────────────────────────────────┘
                            No                        Yes
                ┌──────────────┐   ┌───────────────────────────────────┐
                │ Do not take  │   │ Am I excited and reasonably         │
                │ this action  │   │ nervous about taking this action?   │
                └──────────────┘   └───────────────────────────────────┘
                                    No                        Yes
                        ┌──────────────┐   ┌───────────────────────────────────┐
                        │ Do not take  │   │ TAKE THIS COURAGEOUS ACTION!        │
                        │ this action  │   │                                     │
                        └──────────────┘   └───────────────────────────────────┘
```

Courage

Courage is often connected with people who willingly walk into life-threatening situations. Sometimes it is part of a chosen profession, such as a soldier or a firefighter. Other times, courage is called upon for a single, heroic moment, like a mom rushing into danger to save her child. Other times, it is considered courageous to perform rare feats of adventure, such a climbing Mt. Everest. The people who do these things deserve respect and admiration. I am especially grateful to those who put their lives at risk for me and my freedom. They don't know me, and yet they would save me. Truly amazing.

This book is not about those inspiring people or their incredible sacrifices. This book is about ordinary people making small efforts every day, doing their best to bring something positive into the world. This section about courage is designed to inspire you to perform little acts of courage every day. Small courageous actions repeatedly taken will build your confidence over time. As your confidence grows, so will your courage and the size of your actions. When I was a young adult, making eye contact and smiling at the cashier at the grocery store was a courageous act. Twenty years later, asking my boss for a raise was my level for a courageous act. The bigger your confidence, courage, and actions become, the greater success you will enjoy. You will begin to inspire others. You will begin to lead them - influence them. Your opportunities will multiply. Everyday courage creates a lifetime of opportunities, confidence, and successes.

Contrary to what you might think, courage is not an emotion. I used to think of it as the opposite of fear, but it is not. Fear is an emotion imposed upon you. Courage is an emotional tool within your control. It is a tool you can use to battle and override fear. You will not be able to conquer or eliminate fear - only God can do that - but you can use faith and logic to counter it at any time. We need to distinguish between natural, healthy adrenaline which can promote a great performance and unfavorable fear which can prevent us from stepping out into new arenas to grow, connect, and succeed. Faith and logic are the antidote to fear. Courage is their child.

Faith refers to hope in things unseen, such as in God's eternal plan or your own ability to solve problems. Faith is often manifested in confidence in the present and optimism for the future. Logic, on the other hand, refers to a process your discerning mind goes through to make a determination about truth or risk. Logic helps you decide when to take action. When you create a cycle of action, courage, and confidence, you become more aware of opportunities and more prepared to take advantage of them. You create a cycle of success.

The diagram below shows the cycle of success. All of us go through this process when we are provided with an opportunity. We logically evaluate the opportunity and decide whether to take action or not. If we take action - regardless of its success or failure - we develop a little bit more courage. That courage moves us in the direction of greater confidence - more faith in ourselves. More confidence brings more opportunities and the likelihood of more action, further amplifying our courage and confidence. It is important to note that courage is not required for action. Instead, action is the catalyst for courage. Eventually, this becomes a self-propelling process. If you ever feel trapped or stuck or depressed, take an action. A small action. If that action doesn't help, try a different small action. The attempts will encourage you and guide you to success.

When I was struggling to lose weight after my neck fusion surgery, I was only somewhat successful counting my caloric intake. I was able to sustain it for a few weeks, but I would slide back into bad eating habits. So I decided to try something different. I started walking after dinner.

At first, it was just one or two evenings a week. I found I enjoyed the fresh air and my little bit of time alone so much, I began to walk almost every evening. Then, I added a little jog. Eventually, the back of my legs and bum started looking firmer. That made me really motivated to continue! And since I was moving every day, relieving stress, and feeling better about how I looked, I didn't want to eat as much. The little action of a short walk led to a longer workout which gave me more physical strength, health, and self-confidence. One small action created a cycle of success.

Diagram of the Cycle of Success:

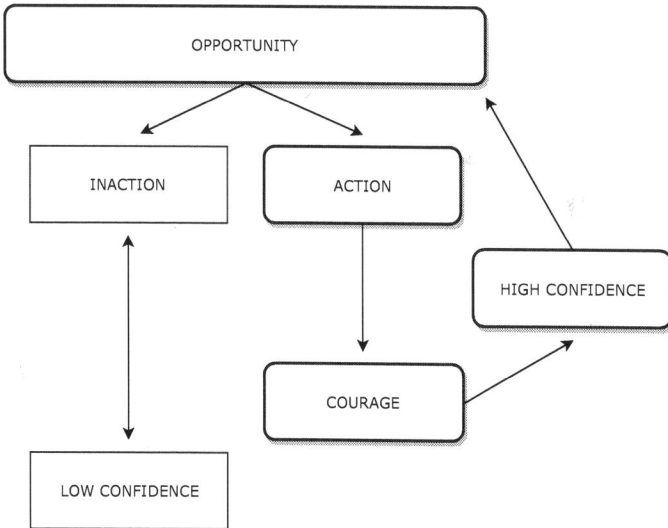

Execution

Creative ideas and passionate mission statements mean nothing if they are not transformed by action and introduced into the world. Once a decision is made, the most difficult part of getting anything done is the hurdle of beginning the very first moment of action. That's why Nike's "Just Do It" campaign was so successful. Most people understand how easy it is to find a million reasons to avoid doing "it" now. Procrastination is easy. Fearless Does do the hard work of creating momentum and executing their plans.

A great way to get started on a big goal is to break it down into little steps. You don't even have to start at the beginning. Just pick the easiest thing you can do and get it done. You will gain both confidence and momentum as you complete each step. It doesn't matter how small the step is - your mind will feel a sense of accomplishment and get a little rush of pride. It will want more. Feed it!

When I began writing this book, I had a general idea of a few of the topics I wanted to write about. I created an outline, picked one topic and started typing words. If I got stuck, I looked up a quote related to the topic to trigger ideas. I also thought about situations in my life related to the topic and began typing my stories. In the beginning, nothing I wrote was cohesive. My outline changed perhaps fifty times. I put no pressure on myself to have it all figured out, or to type a certain number of words, or sit at the computer a certain number of hours. I focused on only two small steps: to type something every day and to email my coach that I typed something that day. Amazingly, once I sat down and started typing, I often ended up with drafts of full paragraphs or pages. Even more amazingly, my book was ready for review in just a few months. One other point...I was not perfect. I had some skip days: days I didn't feel well or I was upset about something or was feeling anxious about a perceived lack of direction. But I didn't give up. I shared my worries with my friends and they talked me through it. I prayed for guidance and I received it. I took control of my negative thoughts, got some fresh air, gave myself some grace, then sat myself back down and typed. If I had given up, you would not be reading my book right now. Please don't give up on your dreams. If I can do it, you can too!

Here are some tips for executing a plan of action:
1. Believe you can do it.
2. You will not have all the confidence you want to make perfect decisions.
3. Make decisions anyway.
4. You will not have all the information you want to create a perfect plan.
5. Create a plan anyway.
6. You will not have all the skills you want to take perfect small bold actions.
7. Take small bold actions anyway.
8. Adjust the plan, as needed.
9. Don't give up!

Much of your success will depend on how many initiatives you can execute to completion. Starting is the hardest part. Just take the first small, bold step.

'Take Bold Steps' Worksheet

Sometimes people make a game out of asking, "If you could go to dinner with anyone who ever lived, who would it be?" Many people answer with a famous politician, actor, or religious leader. Not me. My answer is Captain James T. Kirk of the Starship Enterprise. I know - he's not a real person, he's a TV character. But he is my role model of courage and leadership. He led his team to the successful resolution of every crisis. His mission statement was concise and bold and he repeated it every week so all of us on the couch at home was clear about his vision and purpose.

"Space. The final frontier. These are the voyages of the Starship Enterprise. Its five year mission: to explore strange new worlds, to seek out new life and new civilizations, to boldly go where no man has gone before."

How are they going to accomplish their goals? Boldly! He led them into the unknown using two bold strategies:

1. He exuded confidence that, together, they could solve any problem they faced.
2. He valued diversity and utilized all available skill-sets and resources in creative ways to get the job done.

I encourage you to take some time with your TV, phone, and computer turned off to dream big or think of a way to solve a problem in a creative way. Allow boldness into your imagination. Don't set any limits to your confidence, abilities, or resources. When you have a good idea, no matter how crazy it seems, take one small bold action towards it. Keep taking small bold actions each day and you will gain momentum. Until one day, you realize you are moving at light speed to fulfill your mission. "Live Long and Prosper!"

Write your crazy good idea here:

_____

_____

_____

_____

_____

_____

Describe three small bold actions you will take to gain momentum towards your goal:

1. _____

2. _____

3. _____

Pick one of the small bold actions and do it today!

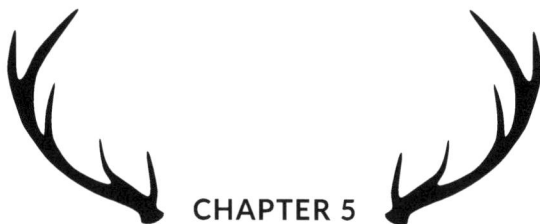

THE SUMMIT: INFLUENTIAL LEADERSHIP

'CHAPTER 5: THE SUMMIT: INFLUENTIAL LEADERSHIP' describes the worldview of a great communicator. I explain successful techniques for creating trust and developing influence with anyone. The various interpersonal skills we discuss are Communication, Curiosity, Awareness, Consideration, and Encouragement. The 'Lead Your Herd' Challenge at the end of the chapter will help you commit the practices of leadership to memory. You will learn to 'Grow a Pair of Antlers' and become a Fearless Doe.

"Great minds discuss ideas; average minds discuss events; small minds discuss people."

— *Eleanor Roosevelt*

Communication

In 1984, Ronald Reagan was running against Walter Mondale for re-election to the Presidency. Mondale was trying to convince the American people that Reagan was too old to continue the job. During one of their debates, the moderator asked Reagan if he had any doubt in his mind that he would have the energy to function during physically difficult circumstances. He replied with a straight face, "Not at all, and I will not make age an issue of this campaign. I am not going to exploit, for political purposes, my opponent's youth and inexperience." Everyone burst into laughter, including Mondale. Ronald Reagan won that election by a landslide, eventually becoming known as "The Great Communicator". He understood his audience and catered his communication content and style to them.

The goal of communication is to facilitate understanding. Your job in every interpersonal interaction is to 1) gain an understanding of the other person's perspective, ideas, and needs and 2) present your perspective, ideas, and needs in a way they can clearly understand.

Communication is the management skill of relationships. It is a set of skills that includes the obvious tasks of listening and talking, but, for greater influence, also requires the proper attitude. Before you enter into a conversation, pause and think about the outcome you would like to achieve. For example, do you place a higher priority on defending your "right" position or do you want to compromise and contribute to a respectful marriage? Your motives will be clear in how you communicate during the conversation.

To communicate for positive results, meet the other person with an attitude of good faith, curiosity, compassion, and humility. Good faith means you expect the best from the other person - that you believe they want the best for you. It means you do not need to get defensive or over-explain your position because you have confidence in the possibilities of an open, honest discussion. Be curious about the other person's feelings, opinions, and needs. Have compassion for their struggles, the pain from their past, and even the hurt you may have caused them. And be humble. It is easy to point out all the ways the other person can improve, how they messed up. The conversation will go better if you focus on how you can improve and how you can fix what you messed up. The tone of your conversation can strengthen your relationship and reinforce the belief you have a partner who has your back. Or, it can weaken the team and break the bonds of trust and respect.

A good communicator also sets expectations and provides timely feedback. Your goal as a leader is to help individuals and teams succeed. These people could be your co-workers, your boss, your family, your friends, or other associates. As a manager, you will set goals and priorities, then provide regular guidance and training for improvement. The same process can be used with your kids to help them learn responsibility. As you invest your efforts into teaching and encouraging someone, they will grow and accomplish things they may not have thought possible. They may get all the credit for those achievements. As an Influential Leader, you get to stand in the back of the room and cheer with the crowd.

Here are some games to play to make effective, influential communication easier:

1. **Game of Ping Pong**. Play this game when you are trying to make a decision with someone and you are not easily coming to an agreement.
   a. To Play:
      i. Bounce perspectives and ideas back and forth with the other person.
   b. The Rules:
      i. Assume there is no truth, only perspective. If you are certain your viewpoint is the truth, you may communicate in a closed-minded and aggressive manner. The other person may respond by shutting down or walking away. A mindset open to change creates productive dialogue.
      ii. Respect each person's perspective as a valid point of view. This attitude enables each person to listen to the other's ideas and opinions and promotes discussion, questions, and decisions
   c. The Win:
      i. You come to an amicable agreement favorable to both people.

2. **Game of Password**. Play this game when you are trying to express your perspective or emotion and you are not feeling understood.
   a. To Play:
      i. Explain your perspective or emotion to try to get the other person to understand it.
      ii. Take turns explaining and understanding each other's points of view.
   b. The Rules:

  i. After you explain your perspective or emotion to the other person, they can either:

   1. Mirror you, which means they repeat your message back to you using their own words, then ask if they understood you correctly.

   2. Or, they can ask you a clarifying question.

  ii. If they ask you a clarifying question, patiently answer it with the goal of helping them understand.

  iii. If they mirror your words, either acknowledge that they understand or explain your perspective in a new way to continue to help them understand.

 c. The Win:

  i. You clearly understand each other's perspective or emotion.

3. **Game of Tag**. Play this game when negative emotions are running high and patience is getting low.

 a. To Play:

  i. First, listen to understand the other person's perspective.

  ii. Then, speak to be understood.

 b. The Rules:

  i. Be direct. Make your point quickly and clearly, but with kindness and consideration. Add more information or analogies only if the other person needs clarification.

  ii. Stay on target. Don't jump around with various points or go on a tangent. Don't dredge up past grievances; simply explain the current issue and possible solutions or approaches to it.

   iii. When an angry thought about the other person comes to mind, take a ten minute break to breathe deeply and remember your priorities. What kind of boss, wife, mother, daughter or friend do you want to be? Return to the conversation as that person.

  c. The Win:

    i. You both feel understood, respected, and cared about.

Curiosity

Curiosity is the fuel that feeds creativity. It is being open to new ideas and pursues learning. Curious people tend to be humble, optimistic, and present in the current moment. They are attentive to the people and situations around them and often see opportunities others miss. Curiosity was the key to my success at growing my business.

When I decided to start a consulting service, I had no idea how I would find clients. Marketing was a scary word to me. It worried me so much, it threatened to stop my entire venture. So I stopped thinking about it and focused on the aspects of the launch that were easier for me. When the time came to obtain clients, I found online resources suggesting I attend a local chamber of commerce meeting.

Donning my most professional business attire and armed with business cards, I was a nervous wreck as I walked into a networking meeting with fifty strangers. They stuck a nametag on me and encouraged me to mingle. Deep breath.

Big smile. Approaching the nearest gentleman, I introduced myself, and asked a few questions. I was genuinely interested in hearing about his business. I was curious. I didn't talk about myself or my new business. I just listened to him, then found a seat for the formal agenda of the meeting. When it was my turn to stand up for thirty seconds and introduce myself, I made up something brief to say then sat back down, working hard to portray confidence the entire time.

After the meeting, the man I spoke with was back by my side faster than I could put my purse on my shoulder. He heard my little spiel and, guess what? He's having a problem with his accounting records. Can I help him? My simple act of curiosity about his business in our first conversation created enough connection between us for him to trust me with his most sensitive information - his finances.

Not long afterwards, I joined another networking organization called Business Network International (BNI). Through their weekly meeting and training sessions, I learned a tremendous amount about sales which improved my skills and my confidence. However, curiosity remains my most successful marketing tool. This isn't a gimmick. I am sincere in my questions and my desire to learn from people and about them. I also share with them information about my business. But I don't stress about it or have to "hard sell" it to them. My curiosity approach to networking is so successful, I often have to turn new clients away.

We generally associate curiosity with scientific research and discovery. It is also, however, a great communication mindset in relationships to quickly establish trust and connection.

Awareness

There is ample conversation around the concept of "being present" in the current moment. Meditation is a wonderful method for calming and focusing the mind through the use of mantras to keep your thoughts in the present moment. Being present is similar to, but is a subset of, being aware. Being present and being aware both represent states of mind in the current moment, but awareness has a much larger scope and can have a much greater impact on your success.

When you are being present, you are focused on one thing. You have turned off all your technology and are single-mindedly paying attention to the one thing going on in your life at that moment. For example, when you are talking with a friend and you are fully engaged in the conversation, you are being present. When you are working 'in the flow' and lose track of time, you are being present. Your mind needs these moments to refresh and recover. We are so busy that we are pushing our brains to constantly multitask or juggle multiple projects. But we are stressing our brains because they can only process one thought at a time. Have you ever tried to juggle three balls in the air? It takes a lot of concentration. Being present is a relaxing break for your brain, so you can feel refreshed and focused on one creative or productive task.

Being aware takes being present to the next level. Being present is focusing on one thing at a time in the here and now, but being aware is attentive to all things in the present moment. A good analogy of how they work together is when you drive a car. You use your forward vision (being present) at the same time as your peripheral vision (being aware) to drive defensively. Another example of this is a manager listening to a suggestion from someone in a meeting while simultaneously observing the subtle emotional responses by the other people in the room. If the manager notices any concerns, she may be able to address and resolve them and keep the project moving forward. The most successful people in life have developed the skills to be present and be aware simultaneously. They are aware of their feelings and those of the people around them. These are Fearless Does.

Isiah Thomas is my favorite basketball player. He is a great example of how to use presence and awareness to lead a championship team. I'm talking about the Isiah that played as a point guard for the Detroit Pistons in the NBA from 1981-1994, not the current young star (although there are many similarities). Isiah (the original) was significantly smaller than the other players. To give you a comparison: Isiah was listed at 6'1" and 180 pounds. Charles Barkley - a peer at the time and of a more typical size - was listed at 6'6" and 252 pounds. Isiah was obviously not the biggest on the court, so he had to develop other abilities. He worked hard on his athletic skills, including focus (presence), speed, and agility. But he also honed his leadership skills, one of which was awareness.

He would bring the ball over the line and wait. He bounced the ball, maybe passed it around a little, and waited and watched. You could see his eyes glancing in every direction and the wheels turning in his head - absorbing and evaluating the situation. Back and forth went the ball - right hand - floor - left hand - floor - right hand - go! He would take off like a jack rabbit to the left, then suddenly dip down low, cut to the right and drive it home, maneuvering through the crowded floor of behemoths. His giant teammates would sometimes step out in front of an opponent to help keep Isiah's path clear. Then he either propelled his body straight up and gently lobbed the ball into the hoop or fired the ball off to a teammate who dunked it in and scored the points. He is considered one of the 50 Greatest Players in NBA History. He was one of the smallest players, but he had the biggest awareness. In my opinion, that was the key to his tremendous success.

You can develop the same skill of awareness in your life to experience championship-level success as a manager, leader, mother, wife, or friend. Practice awareness in each moment. Know what is going on around you. What is each family member doing? If they are not home, where are they? How are you feeling right now? What would you like to be doing? What's going well, what can be improved? Could someone around you use a smile or an encouraging word right now?

Being present is the first step to being aware, so put down your phone, close your email and internet browser, and look at the person in front of you. Give them your full attention. Then, be aware of what is going on around you and in the lives and hearts of those you lead and care about. Awareness will create a deeper connection with others and improve your relationships.

Consideration

To be considerate is to think about the well-being of another person. Not to the detriment to yourself, but to the benefit of both. Being considerate of others is the baseline for successful leadership and teamwork. It is the foundation for respect and loyalty in your relationships, especially a marriage. Consideration, or lack thereof, sets the tone of conversation in our society - whether it is in our political discussions or our social media posts.

A considerate person is empathetic, generous with their time and attention, thoughtful, compassionate, and supportive. They respect the needs and feelings of others and consider them to be as important as their own. They stop and think about how their words and actions will affect others. They find ways to bring happiness and encouragement to others.

Consideration of another's needs and feelings is, perhaps, the most important way to show them you care about them. You do not have to agree with someone to care about them. We are all living on a big, spinning ball in the middle of nowhere. We are each doing the best we can with what we have been given - from our past and in our environment. Unfortunately, we have some hurting and unstable people on the planet who cause some really big problems. Bigotry, abuse, and terrorism are all results of fear, pain, and a lack of hope. These people can be pitied, but their behaviors should not be tolerated. But most of us are ordinary people who are hurting and scared and in desperate need of love and acceptance. If we did not receive this as a child, our pain may show itself in our adult relationships as defensiveness or passive-aggressive behavior. We may feel jealousy or be over-sensitive to comments or perceived slights. We all crave people in our lives to be considerate of our feelings and needs. The irony is that it is such an easy gift to give someone. All it requires is a small act of kindness, a few minutes of empathy, a hug, a thank-you, or a word of encouragement.

When you are connecting with, understanding, or relating to what another person is feeling, you are being empathetic. It is difficult to do that unless you truly care about the other person and are curious about their circumstances and desires. A considerate person, like a curious one, asks a lot of questions and is an active listener. When you actively listen to someone, with attention and compassion, they will trust you and want to continue to develop their connection with you.

Active listening means you are curious about what someone is going through and are asking questions which demonstrate interest and keep the conversation going. Active listening means you are loving them compassionately. You are not judging them because they made a mistake. You are not defending yourself or your viewpoints when they are describing how you hurt them or explaining how they disagree with you. You are not thinking about what you are going to say next. You are only mirroring what they said in your own words and asking clarifying questions to show them you were listening. You could also build on their ideas if it's a brainstorming session to solve a problem or make a decision. You can offer encouragement or ideas or options. But only offer advice if asked for, and state it very tactfully and lovingly with respect and kindness.

Consideration is not limited to your family and close friends. We are called to love everyone - neighbors, coworkers, strangers, even enemies. Being considerate of their needs and demonstrating good manners are the most effective ways to offer a little kindness. A basic example of consideration for a stranger is holding the door open for the delivery man whose arms are full of packages.

Another way to be considerate is to refrain from gossip. If you have a problem with someone, take it directly to them and be honest. Tell them you want to resolve the issue, listen to their side of the story, share your side, and try to work it out. Not all problems can be solved. You may need to disengage from the relationship if they are not willing to work with you in good faith. But keep others out of it. Keep it between the two of you. And put in your best effort to show you care about them as much as you want them to care about you.

Our tone on social media has become inconsiderate. It is so easy for us to berate someone we are not looking at in the eyes, especially a stranger we will never meet. A good way to assess if you should hit the send button on your message is to imagine how you would feel if you were on the receiving end of your comment. You can disagree with someone, but do it with consideration for the other person's feelings and with respect for their point of view. If you are thinking about responding via social media to someone who is making racial slurs or other bigoted comments, don't even bother. They will not listen to you and any comment you make will just inflame the conversation. You are better off allowing their comments to disappear into the wind. Without a reaction, a bully will eventually go away. If you are following someone who doesn't bring you joy and motivation, unfollow them!

Encouragement

Have you ever noticed that the root of the word encouragement is courage? By encouraging someone, you are giving them a boost of courage. Do not underestimate the power of this in another's life. Have you worked for a boss who was always demanding and rarely appreciated you? They were not being encouraging. Have you had a friend who was always complaining and dumping their frustrations on you, but was rarely there to support you? They were not being encouraging. Did you want to keep working at that job or spending your precious time with that "friend"? No! Of course not.

Encouragement is an act of love and kindness. We want this - and deserve it - from the people in our lives. Even if you don't yet feel very confident in yourself, you know deep down inside you deserve better.

I was near the end of a hike the other day and I must have looked worn out. I had enjoyed my time on the trail, but the last section was an uphill climb during the heat of the afternoon. As I was approaching an older couple who were passing in the other direction, the man said to me, "You can do it!" Then the woman said, "This…coming from the man who keeps asking to turn around!" He immediately looked down to avoid eye contact with me. I could see the hurt and embarrassment her comment caused him. This brief moment made me realize how much damage can be done in just a few words. The juxtaposition of his encouraging words against her discouraging words made the point even more clear. Communication with other people should be honest and kind. We have the power to bolster other people's confidence…to help them accomplish more and feel better about themselves. Sometimes, it only takes a few encouraging words.

When you have an encouraging approach, you set clear expectations and follow-up with timely feedback and guidance. You are honest with people and your discussions have no hidden agendas. The words you choose are kind, compassionate and energizing. You address problems head-on, listen to others' points of view, and give and accept grace.

If you work on my team and make a mistake, you will hear, "We all make mistakes. Let's work together to come up with a plan to fix it and learn from it." If it's a big mistake, I may have to address it formally, but it's up to them to take the opportunity to learn and do better the next time. It's important to remember your feedback is designed to influence their future behavior. It's not your responsibility to make the other person change or be happy. Their response to your feedback is in their control. But it can be difficult to accept what we cannot control. Occasionally, you must end a dysfunctional relationship to avoid being caught in the aggravating and exhausting Whirlpool of Control.

Diagram of the Whirlpool of Control:

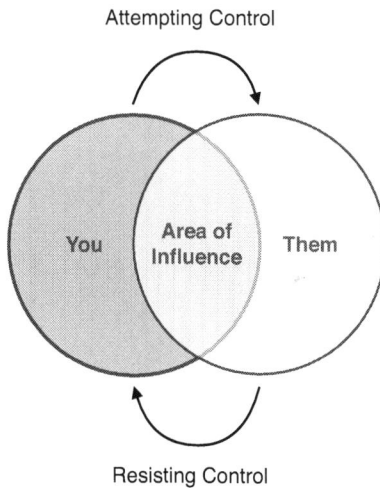

Attempting Control

You | Area of Influence | Them

Resisting Control

Encouragers must keep in mind the old adage (modified to this book's theme): You can lead a Doe to water, but you can't make her drink!

However, when you are in the Area of Influence and are encouraging someone, you can expect the best from them. They will listen to your advice and absorb your courage. They will thrive on your team and pass the encouragement on.

'Lead Your Herd' Challenge

Make a commitment to 'Grow a Pair of Antlers' by practicing the values, attitudes and skills described in "The Fearless Climb to Lead Your Herd" for 25 days.

1. Sign and date below to take the 'Lead Your Herd' Challenge.
2. Do the following actions each day and check them off the list as you finish them.
3. Post your take-away and/or small bold action from each category at www.TheFearlessClimb.com/growapairofantlers.

I agree to do one of the following action groups each day for the next 25 days.

Signature _____

Date _____

- **Days 1-5: Ch. 1: Freedom, Integrity, Wisdom, Fear, Faith**
  - Re-read one of the categories from Chapter 1
  - My take-away from the category is _____
  - My small bold action today will be _____

- **Days 6-10: Ch. 2: Humility, Creativity, Indomitable Will, Flexibility, Resilience**
  - Re-read one of the categories from Chapter 2
  - My take-away from the category is _____
  - My small bold action today will be _____

- **Days 11-15: Ch. 3: Responsibility, Connection, Purpose, Legacy, Lifestyle**
  - Re-read one of the categories from Chapter 3
  - My take-away from the category is _____
  - My small bold action today will be _____

- **Days 16-20: Ch. 4: Optimism, Confidence, Decisiveness, Courage, Execution**
  - Re-read one of the categories from Chapter 4
  - My take-away from the category is _____
  - My small bold action today will be _____

- **Days 21-25: Ch. 5: Communication, Curiosity, Awareness, Consideration, Encouragement**
  - Re-read one of the categories from Chapter 5
  - My take-away from the category is _____
  - My small bold action today will be _____

CONCLUSION

THE FEARLESS DOE EDITION of this book is devoted to inspiring and empowering women. This is not a book about feminism or equality. It is a book about new opportunities and how to embrace them. It is about respecting and celebrating our differences. We do not, in any social movement, have to put someone else down to rise up. We can be kind and respectful to a person of any race, religion, or orientation. We can create connection with eye contact, a smile, and curiosity about other worldviews and experiences. We can collaborate on solutions and work as a team to create a new norm in our society.

What is true at a societal level is also true at a corporate level. Those of us who are entrepreneurs and CEOs can choose to manage our businesses with integrity. We can pay fair and equal wages for an employee of any race or gender. We can reduce economic class differences by providing job opportunities with more generous living wages and benefits. We can reframe the goals of our businesses to better support the needs of our families. We need to think about what we can bring into the world for the benefit of humanity. It starts with thinking about how we can benefit the person across the table from us.

Every person has a struggle and a desire to be loved and accepted. To truly create a better life for ourselves, the judgements, hypocrisies, and the power plays must end. We are not better or worse than someone else, but we also are not equal. By design, we are each unique and special. Only our capacity to love and be loved is equal because it emanates from a higher power. Love is our common ground and we can use it to make the world a better place for everyone.

The information in this book can help anyone on his or her personal and professional journey through life. However, I focused on speaking to women because we have few role models who have successfully forged a way through our complex modern lifestyle. We also have limited resources for guidance on navigating our path to the summit of leadership. I hope we will start sharing our stories to enlighten, support, and inspire each other.

We have had so many new opportunities open up to us over the past few decades, but are still struggling to decide what is best for us and our family. Often, our choices are critiqued by our parents and friends, so we become uncertain that we have made the right ones. Then we still have to figure out how to manage all our responsibilities in our homes and at the office. Advice about how to create a "balanced" life is prolific, but achieving it is impossible. Every day can feel like a monotonous whirlwind where peace and joy become elusive. We are juggling more, exhausted more, and doubting ourselves more. Since our lifestyles are so different from our mothers', we find it difficult to gauge whether we are being good wives, mothers, daughters, and friends. We feel pressure to do it all successfully, without looking tired or anxious or fat or old.

This has created new dynamics in the relationship between a man and a woman. The stress is negatively impacting our marriages as our husbands are also struggling to define new family roles and become partners in raising the children and managing the household. I have empathy for the lifestyle changes men are also trying to navigate. Any conversation we have about how to resolve conflict and simplify our lives must include both people.

But for the purposes of this book, I simply wanted to share the struggles I have experienced as a modern, liberated woman and try to offer some ideas to other women about how to succeed in this brave, new world. I am not advocating a return to the days where women had limited or no options and rights. I treasure my freedom to vote, learn, and pursue my interests. There are still many women today who long for, but are denied, these opportunities. And while I acknowledge we still have progress to make, many women now have freedoms previously unimaginable. And perhaps that is our conundrum. We don't want to complain about the challenges of the modern woman's life for fear of sounding unappreciative. But if we don't talk about the issues and share ideas for handling them, we will continue to struggle.

Women have a wonderful new opportunity to "Grow a Pair of Antlers" and work closely with men to make a positive difference in the world. Equality should not be an adversarial term. Instead, let it represent the diverse members of a talented team who treat one another with respect to solve problems and make meaningful progress and a big impact together.

Let's work together to create something greater using our individual talents and passions. Success is at the intersection of our dreams. I wrote this book to encourage women to bring their unique abilities and perspectives into the world with Intentional Purpose and Courageous Actions. I wrote this book to celebrate our journey, our Fearless Climb, to the summit of Influential Leadership.

Congratulations to all of you who are ready to "Grow a Pair of Antlers" and make the world a better place!

'Intention Journal' Guide

Get a composition notebook or journal and keep it by your bed. Every morning, date the top of a new page then take a few minutes to write what you want most in your life. Write your dreams as if you have already achieved them. Include emotions. Write down how you will feel when you have accomplished your goals. Also write about who you are helping and why to stay connected to your purpose.

Go crazy with it. Don't judge or limit the possibilities. Write quickly, but as detailed as possible. Fill an entire page with descriptive words and emotions. Then close it up until tomorrow. When you open your journal the next morning, do not look at the prior day's journals. Write what is in your heart today on a new page. You will find that some things will change over time. Others will repeat with more accuracy and clarity.

Let the clarity come through your exploration. Don't try to force it. The vision is already inside of you, you just need to let it slip past the logical filters of your brain. You will know you have found it when you feel passionate about the possibilities and excited to get started.

Believe that by the time you get to the end of the journal book, you will have what you want. Don't worry about how you will get it, the universe will take care of that. All you need to do is believe that your dreams will be realized and the path will be provided.

When you are done writing, ask yourself, "What's next?" This is a prompt to think about what to do today to take a step towards fulfilling your dreams. Start browsing the internet to learn how other people have achieved similar goals. Read books and take online courses. Hire a coach. Save images and words and quotes to your phone and make them your wallpaper. Create a vision board and hang it on your wall. Visualize what you want and ignore what you don't want in your life. Intentionally and courageously begin your climb and trust your instincts.

Appendix B

'Stay on Your Path' Worksheet

Here are the steps for creating a plan of action and executing it:

1. Create a plan of action based on your vision, purpose, and mission statement. Your plan should be a bullet-point list with one big goal, a few major milestones, and a list of small bold actions you need to take to achieve each milestone.
2. Add due dates to the big goal and to one milestone.
3. Pick one small bold action listed under the dated milestone and do it today.
4. Keep taking small bold actions until you reach the dated milestone.
5. Add a due date to another milestone.
6. Repeat Steps 3-5 until you reach the big goal.

Stay on Your Path Worksheet

Mission Statement (from the 'Plan Your Mission' Worksheet):

_____

_____

_____

_____

One Big Goal: Due Date:_____

_____

_____

_____

_____

1. **Milestone:**   Due Date: _____

_____

_____

_____

_____

a. Small Bold Action: Due Date: _____

_____

_____

_____

_____

b. Small Bold Action: Due Date: _____

_____

_____

_____

_____

c. Small Bold Action: Due Date: _____

_____

_____

_____

_____

2. **Milestone:**   Due Date: _____

_____

_____

_____

_____

a. Small Bold Action: Due Date: _____

_____

_____

_____

_____

_____

b. Small Bold Action: Due Date: _____

_____

_____

_____

_____

c. Small Bold Action: Due Date: _____

_____

_____

_____

_____

3. **Milestone:**   Due Date: _____

_____

_____

_____

_____

a. Small Bold Action: Due Date: _____

_____

_____

_____

_____

_____

b. Small Bold Action: Due Date: _____

_____

_____

_____

_____

_____

c. Small Bold Action: Due Date: _____

_____

_____

_____

_____

_____

A Man's Perspective

I am a baby boomer who grew up in a "traditional" household. My Dad had a full-time job and occasional part-time jobs to make ends meet. My mom ran the house, that itself being a full-time job with five kids. My grandparents were the depression-era generation, so in a sense my parents grew up in traditional households too. Can you believe that we are less than 100 years out from the Great Depression? Can you see how different home life is today than it was 100 years ago, and how much the traditions have changed?

When Kathleen and I were soon to be wed, we began a search for our new home. We found a place that we both loved but was above the original budget that we had in mind. Fortunately, we both had established careers and a very nice combined income. Neither income alone would be able to support us if we bought that house. So, I asked Kathleen a very simple question: *Do you plan to continue working, or do you want to become a stay-at-home mom?*

Kathleen's answer was clear and definitive: She loved her

work and the mental stimulation that it brought. She has always wanted to grow and learn, and her career gave her the perfect platform for that. She also loved being a mom, so she did not want to give that up. She was essentially committing to two full-time jobs, one in the home and one outside.

I listened to the part of her answer I wanted to hear: we can afford the house. What I did not realize until recently, was that I didn't listen to the whole answer. She wanted BOTH. We were committing to a big monthly mortgage that would lock us both into full-time paying jobs. But what about the home front? I had failed to ask a very important second question of myself: *Would I step up my commitment in the marriage to allow her the freedom to have both roles, to experience a happy work life and a happy home life?*

I knew it would have been wrong of me to make her fulfill both full-time roles alone, so I stepped it up to help on many time-consuming chores in the household. I cook. I clean. I do laundry. I buy groceries. I shuttle kids around. These things are all helpful, but I could sense that there was something missing. After any given exhausting day at work, all I wanted to do when I came home was sit and relax but I knew there was work to be done. I would crank through all of my household chores and crash on the recliner. After Kathleen worked just as hard as me all day and did her home chores too, she still wasn't done. I would hear her helping the kids with homework or a friend with a personal issue, helping an elderly relative with their taxes or coordinating a household move, etc. She was still trudging on, and I was done for the day. That stirred strong feelings of guilt in me, but I took no action. Her extra chores were sometimes her heaviest burden, and I was absent. The best I could muster was guilt.

I am a stubborn guy. The roots of my stubbornness may be related to my being male, or maybe not. Regardless, my stubborn streak is a hindrance to my own growth. To share more of Kathleen's burden, I needed to grow. Growth is not comfortable, and I really, really like comfort.

I am now a less stubborn guy and growing. What motivated the change wasn't an argument, a touching romantic comedy, or anything external. My motivations had to come from within. I'm convinced that is the only way for stubbornness to be defeated. I had to choose change, not have it thrust upon me. I had to find my "why". Why should I change?

My "why" is rooted in what I want out of life. I want a wife that loves me. I want kids that look up to me. I want to play with my future grandkids. Simply put, I want to be happy and have fun. Happiness is an active emotion that must be constantly cultivated. I choose to direct my energies toward cultivating that happiness in me and those around me.

The seed of my happiness is humility. I acknowledge that I can do things better and can take on a larger role in the family. I will adapt and be flexible. I'm not my father and I don't live in his time, so there is no disgrace in the discovery that the role I have played is not the role I must play.

The disgrace would be to fail to act nobly with that new knowledge. I viewed my stubbornness as strength, resolve, conviction, and many other complementary ways. I'm sure I am not alone in this interpretation, but that doesn't make it right. It is time for men to find a new strength: humility. Do the right thing, even when nobody's watching (but someone always is).

By Ed Jubenville

About Eleanor Roosevelt

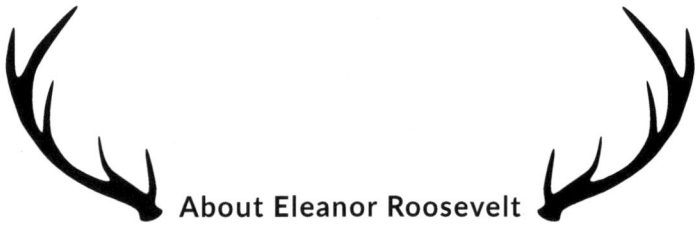

You may have noticed most of the quotes in this book were from Eleanor Roosevelt. She was the wife of Franklin D. Roosevelt, the American President from 1933-1945. Eleanor redefined the role of First Lady and seized the opportunity to champion civil rights and women's rights through press conferences, lectures, radio broadcasts, and a daily newspaper column. She also helped draft the "Universal Declaration of Human Rights", adopted by the United Nations in 1948. Here is one of her astute observations I am amazed is still relevant today:

"Too often the great decisions are originated and given form in bodies made up wholly of men, or so completely dominated by them that whatever of special value women have to offer is shunted aside without expression."

— Eleanor Roosevelt

It is way past time men and women of every race start working together for a common purpose, honoring the diversity that makes us better as a whole. Let's begin a peaceful, but powerful movement focused on love and service to each other that is founded on respect for our uniqueness and connection in our humanity. Let's join together for the benefit of our families, our health, and our happiness to develop new rules for flexible work schedules, fair pay rates, and career development. Let's redefine entrepreneurship from a way to make lots of money for the owner to 'a business venture designed to create jobs that support families and serve employees with consideration for their well-being.' The owner still deserves to earn the big bucks, but the purpose of the business should shift to serve others. Now that would be Fearless Leadership!

About the Author

Kathleen Ries-Jubenville is a financial management and leadership expert. She has been a consultant and trainer to hundreds of entrepreneurs and specializes in developing and implementing tech-savvy management and accounting systems designed to free the business owner from the daily grind. The benefits to the business are efficiency and scalability, which ultimately increases profitability.

Kathleen has a business degree in finance and is a Certified QuickBooks ProAdvisor. Prior to going into business for herself, she worked in corporate positions ranging from local home construction companies to international financial securities management organizations.

She left her job after her second baby was born and started a part-time, home-based bookkeeping service to gain more control and flexibility over her time and responsibilities. The business grew quickly and Kathleen became an early adopter of cloud technologies to expand through delegation. As her knowledge and experience grew, she also regularly served in high-level executive roles on a part-time basis.

She has a broad range of experience consulting with entrepreneurs at various stages of business development

- from start-up adventurers to CEOs of established corporations. This has enabled her to quickly identify opportunities for any business executive to lead their company into more profitable growth. She learned she could apply the same principles to a business of any size or industry and achieve similar positive results.

One pattern Kathleen noticed in many companies was a lack of mentorship for the management team and their staff in the skills of high performance, integrity, and professionalism. The shortage of role models is especially challenging for women who are trying to figure out how to juggle a career and their family responsibilities. So Kathleen decided to write this book and is creating video content, webinars, and online courses to supplement her ongoing coaching and consulting services.

Kathleen lives in beautiful Orange County, California with her husband, Ed, two young adult children, Kaitlyn and John, and their two cats, Buzz and Shadow.

Grow a Pair of Antlers
The Fearless Climb to Lead Your Herd

The Fearless Doe Edition
Intentional * Courageous * Influential

Free downloadable resources are available at
www.TheFearlessClimb.com

Acknowledgments

I would like to thank my dear friends who have supported me on my journey: Paul and Natalie Spitzzeri, Craig and Tina Javid, Paul and Annamae Huante, Bill and Sue Mills, Paula Moyer, Jim Ries, and the Jones Family: Roberta, Randy, Dawnita, and Danny.

I would also like to thank the following organizations and their leaders for encouraging me to pursue new adventures and achieve greater levels of success:

Brett A. Blair is the President and Peak Performance Coach of Best Life Global. He is creating a Best Life Movement by hosting monthly workshops and an annual Best Life Summit. Brett helped me clarify my dreams and craft a plan to share my message authentically with the world. With his guidance, friendship, and support, I went from feeling I was on the "treadmill of life" to publishing my first book (a lifelong dream) and pivoting my career to make a bigger, more fulfilling, impact in the world. You can connect with Brett at www.BestLifeGlobal.com and on social media sites. Brett's motivational book, "From Autopilot to Authentic" is available at www.Amazon.com.

Mary Belden-McGrath is the Chief Relationship Officer and Experiential Leadership Trainer at DrivenLeadership. I attended her weekend program called BOLD Advanced Leadership. It pushed me into a deeper connection with my unique point of view and taught me to love and support others with greater compassion, humility, and energy. I also met an incredible group of people who gave their best to me and to each other. Mary showed us how to go "ALL IN!". For more information about the BOLD experience, go to www.DrivenForLife.com. Mary also published a beautiful journal workbook called "Some Day is Now", available at www.Amazon.com.

Brad C. Wenneberg, Shihan, is a 7th Degree Black Belt (Kyoshi) and the Founder of the American Martial Arts Academy (AMAA) in Orange County, California. Shihan, his family and their wonderful team of trainers are committed to teaching the highest degree of integrity and discipline at physical levels appropriate to your age and personal challenges. Every person on staff cares deeply about the success of each individual and safety is a priority. Kids and adults all feel welcome and have a great time. Their website is www.KarateOC.com. Shihan Wenneberg's inspirational book, "Unleash Your Inner Warrior", is listed on www.Amazon.com.

Eastside Christian Church is a faith-based community of people who are in various stages in their spiritual journey. Eastside's vision is "to transform our homes, community and world by pursuing God, building community and unleashing compassion, one neighborhood at a time." The church has several campuses, but it also live streams services and archives the messages on their website, www.Eastside.com.

Made in the USA
San Bernardino, CA
10 October 2018